ADVANCE

"*Burn Notice* will awaken a ... n your life. As you read the power... k, you will find your heart burning to serve Jesus with every breath that you have. Read this book prayerfully, and then go all-in on God's assignment for your life! Thank you, Aaron, for inspiring a generation to live for a higher purpose."

—**Randy Lawrence Jr.**, president of Messenger College and author of *The Burn Factor* and *In Pursuit*

"A call to a 'go beyond the walls' Christianity. You will enjoy reading about all God has done as Aaron shares many personalized stories of God's power and goodness for those willing to take a risk to follow Him. With a raw and contagious affection for Christ, Aaron lays out an inspirational call to leave what is comfortable and find our God-given *Burn Notice*."

—**Jeremie Bridges**, senior pastor of The Canopy Ministries

"Aaron's masterful work of balancing captivating thoughts while taking you on a journey to ignite the passion of Christ is truly amazing. You and I were made for mighty, Kingdom purposes. Looking for a book that keeps your attention, easy to read, relatable, and filled with encouragement on the next steps of obedience? Then look no further than *Burn Notice*."

—**Kenan Klein**, student and worship leader of Christian Church of Carl Junction

"*Burn Notice* lights a fire under the reader to fulfill the main mission of the great commission, 'Go and do!' Read this book with your shoes on. If you have any spark inside you to do more with the gifts given, then *Burn Notice* is the fuel that will transform you into a fire starter for the lost and dying hordes of humanity!"

—**Don Allen**, president of The Midwest Healing Centers, author, and host of Christ The Healer TV

"Not only does this book inspire the mature in Christ, the way it is written awakens those sleeping from their slumber and brings back to life those who were once dead."

—**Howie Nunnelly**, lead pastor of Impact Church and news anchor ABC/KODE-12

"*Burn Notice* appeals for every Christian to contagiously burn for God wherever they are in order to ignite change and revival in this dark world."

—**Sarah Hayhurst**, chief editor of Sarah Hayhurst LLC

"Aaron gives a fresh take on the familiar theme of living with purpose. His enthusiasm for a life lived in radical obedience to Christ is contagious. And I've witnessed firsthand the immeasurable ripple effect within our community as Aaron seeks the will of God, obeys wholeheartedly, and calls others to do the same."

—**Dr. Travis Hurley**, director of advancement of Watered Gardens Ministries

Burn Notice

BURN
NOTICE

Recognizing Your Most Inner-Fire Purpose

A.M. GARCIA

NASHVILLE

NEW YORK • LONDON • MELBOURNE • VANCOUVER

Burn Notice

Recognizing Your Most Inner-Fire Purpose

Published in New York, New York, by Morgan James Publishing. Morgan James is a trademark of Morgan James, LLC. www.MorganJamesPublishing.com

Unless otherwise noted, all Scripture was taken from the New King James Version®. Copyright © 1982 by Thomas Nelson. Used by permission. All rights reserved.

ISBN 9781642799446 paperback
ISBN 9781642799453 eBook
Library of Congress Control Number: 2019957987

Cover Design by:
Christopher Kirk
www.GFSstudio.com

Interior Design by:
Chris Treccani
www.3dogcreative.net

Morgan James is a proud partner of Habitat for Humanity Peninsula and Greater Williamsburg. Partners in building since 2006.

Get involved today! Visit
MorganJamesPublishing.com/giving-back

To my beautiful, supportive wife. You will never understand enough the outcry of my heart. Without you being my better half, I would not even remotely be a percent of the man I am today.

To the body of Christ, this journal here is to stir up the gift that is inside you for the upward call of God in your lives. Let's change this world forever—together.

Acknowledgments

I would like to personally thank every mentor, leader, teacher, and pastor who has been an influential aspect of my writing career. The fingerprints that every individual has had on my life is a textured addition to who I have become. My thanks to literary agent, Michael Ebeling, for landing the plane with my publishing company, Morgan James Publishing. To my family who has supported and encouraged me on my journey, thank you for believing in me. To the leaders of S.O.S. Ministries, may God continue to increase what He breathed into existence. For everyone else I am trying to accumulate in my thoughts, you know who you are. Let's continue to shape the world with the beauty and nature of God Who gave us life!

FOREWORD

There are moments in your life that mark you. Moments in which you realize that everything from that day forward will change. As odd as it may sound, my moment took place in the gymnasium on our college campus.

I grew up in church, and as a high schooler at camp one summer, I felt God's tug on my heart to give my life to His work. I didn't know what that looked like or what that meant, so I did what any well-meaning high school student would do — I enrolled at a Christian college. It only made sense that if God was calling me to lead His church, I would need some sort of formal training. Although I knew nothing about college, I assumed I would certainly need to be able to answer the difficult theological questions that church goers would ask. The problem was I had grown up in a broken home with problems that would have seemingly disqualified many for ministry.

I was the son of an absent, alcoholic father and of a single mom who was doing whatever she could to make ends meet in order to raise us the best she could in less than ideal circumstances. Not only were the odds not in my favor, if I were to graduate from college, I would be the first grandchild in my whole family to accomplish that goal. In my mind, there was no way I could attain the call that God had placed on my life without the knowledge to be able to lead people toward the God Who had saved me.

Education, not passion, was the problem. Experiencing abuse from my stepfather, having no relationship with my biological father, and being the man of the house at the age of fourteen lit a fire in my heart to see others experience the Heavenly Father change them the same way He had changed me. I had a passion for the fatherless. I had a passion for the abused. I had a passion for the homeless. I had a passion for the addicted. *What I didn't have was the expertise to lead God's church.*

Along with the lack of education, were my insecurities. I questioned whether or not God could truly use a broken kid with little education to teach others about His grace and truth. How would I be able to lead others if I didn't have the answers myself? So, logically — in my mind, college would give me the knowledge I needed to *do ministry.* Surely if I graduated with a ministry degree, I would finally be qualified to lead other people to Jesus – maybe even see God change and transform them!

It was at that point, a year and a half into my college education, that God changed my perspective. I was headed to the gym one chilly night for a game of pickup basketball. The jog across campus was going to be cold, so I threw on my favorite hoodie. (Everybody has a favorite hoodie.) I ran inside the doors of the gym, met up with the guys that were there to play that night, and needed to run in to use the bathroom before the pick-up game got under way.

I walked into the empty bathroom, only to be caught off guard by a man at the sink holding all his possession in a plastic bag, washing his face with the water he had cupped in his hands. He had discovered a time each evening in which the gym was open, but the bathroom was empty. This gave him the opportunity to do the best he could to clean off the dirt from a life of living on the streets. Like the side plot of a film playing in my mind, it was in that moment that God reminded me of the flame He lit in me as a high schooler to give my life to His purpose and His calling. Without thinking, I took off my favorite hoodie, walked over to the man, handed it to him, and shared with him that I wanted him to have it.

Before you think this is a story of me sharing my heroics . . . I awkwardly walked out of the bathroom that night and chose to take a cold walk back to my dorm instead of heading in to join the guys in the pickup basketball game. I will always remember that walk because I didn't feel better about myself. It was odd . . . I thought that giving him my hoodie would make me feel better about myself, but it didn't. I was spending all my energy trying to educate myself on what it would look like to lead others to Christ, and yet I had no idea what to say to the man in the bathroom. It was a moment in which God revealed to me that my call to love others, to share His hope with others, and to minister to others wasn't about God wanting me to *change them*, but rather it was about God wanting to *change me*.

Could it be that God's call on our lives to get outside the walls of the church aren't about whether or not we are educated, equipped, or qualified to share His love with those around us? Could it be that the journey He is calling us to is much more about how He can change us? This was my burn notice. And it changed me forever.

Cody Walker
Lead Pastor, Hope City Church

TABLE OF CONTENTS

INTRODUCTION

I had found myself encapsulated inside a four- by eight-foot walk-in closet. Overwhelmed by what I had experienced the weekend prior, I dropped my bags and had the increasingly emotional thought of, *Was I going to go back to my old life?*

Most people would push away the emotional turmoil, but for me, this was reality. Was I going to go back to my old life, never experiencing a new one, or would I endure reckless faith with no idea where I was going? I had to find out.

"Do I have purpose?" is likely the most self-searched question in all of humanity. Why are we here? Do we mean something? Is there more to this life? Of course, I have a lot of questions myself, but I have even more curiosity. If I was going to find the answer to my questions, I had to explore.

Asking yourself "Do I have purpose?" is like asking yourself "Do you have air in your lungs?" The answer is, undoubtingly, yes. So, if breath gives life, then purpose portrays meaning. It's that simple.

I want to perform an experiment here. I want to formulate a case study that concludes there are no limitations to this life, and we have permission to go further, deeper, and higher than ever before. Don't worry, you won't have to apply to some elite university, nor will you have to rack your brain in the books for hours at a time, and most certainly you won't have to put on that silly lab coat because this case study is all about—*you.*

For far too long, we humans have fabricated the truth that we can't accomplish things in life nor reach further than our logical thinking can take us. Does this seem familiar? It's because we have underestimated ourselves and placed ourselves in a box of comfortability, not knowing what lurks on the outside of limitless possibility. But we are searching—searching for that gift and attempting to find our purpose but falling short every time.

Many of us have found God, giving our lives fully to Him only to find ourselves stuck in the same situations with the same outcomes. Nowhere. But life didn't begin before the resurrection. It began *after* the resurrection when we said yes to Jesus by putting on the full armor of God and when we were given a life of success and purpose. But what is purpose, and how can we obtain it? If I have a calling on my life, what is it? And how do I get there? With all those questions resonating in the back of your mind, and a good probability you picked up this book to find it, this is your chance. This is your moment. Everyone has an "aha" moment. So, this is your "aha" encounter.

After I completed my first novel *Coincidence or God?* The Lord down poured this book into my lap. Now, supernatural instances have happened, and I want to reveal these things to you. Be prepared. There will be testimonies in this book so profound and supernatural that you will see the hand of God working throughout the chapters. Page by page testimonies, teachings, and illustrations that will equip you for your purpose. After all, isn't life more than just a mist that appears for little while and then vanishes (James 4:14)?

Whether you realize it or not, there is a fire on the inside just pressing to get out. I want you to visualize a pilot that is constantly on. It gets just enough fuel to keep the light on. But when the pilot light is given more power and gas, it turns into an inferno, blazing in the visualization of others. People are drawn to it. They are comforted by it. And reluctantly, that inferno has no other desire but to burn–burn with compassion, burn with intention, reflecting onto others and becoming contagious. This is what the book is meant for: to recognize this burn that is within you and to release it to the world that is void without it.

When you acknowledge and recognize this passion within you, this is where *Burn Notice* takes off. I want to reveal more to you right now, but I will lay out the blueprint throughout this book. It's going to be a journey, so come prepared. We will test the heart, siphon out what moves you, and produce passion that will reach full capacity because you have a gift, and it is my responsibility to see that characteristic come to the surface. If you do not reveal your purpose, the world will constantly be void without it. So, are you ready? Ready to burn like never before? Strap in because this is where your life is about to begin. Let's burn to change this world forever. Follow me.

CHAPTER 1:
On Earth as It is in Heaven

I will never forget the first time I stepped foot on spiritual soil. I could tell it was spiritual by the insurmountable emotions I was feeling. We had just arrived by plane in Atlanta, Georgia. This was not my first rodeo as I used to live in Georgia when I was a child, but this time was different. Much different. A close group of us friends had decided to attend a conference. But this was not your typical sit-in-your-seat assembly—this was an actual encounter with heaven. As I attempted to wrap my mind around what was happening, I just filed in line behind the thousands of like-minded individuals in front of me. But I couldn't see the front. All I saw was an epicenter of evangelists, leaders, teachers, and the like. What I had pictured was a canvas of blades of grass all being pushed in the same direction by the wind, which you can't typically see.

The doors had finally opened to the event. It was as if the dam had opened and the rushing waters came pouring into the colosseum. We were greeted by volunteers with lanyards wrapped around their necks. They were smiling, engaged, and lovely. What was their main focus? To greet us with a warm welcome. I could feel the atmosphere of centeredness. I could palpably feel we were all connected. As our group made our way to the seats, we were overwhelmed with joy. We began chatting back and forth, talking nonstop about our feelings and the flights of ideas we were having. Man, was my mind on hyper-drive.

Suddenly the lights shut off. All you could hear were voices. Whispers and shouts. Nothing that produced fear. More like, something bursting on the inside with nowhere to go but out. Instantaneously the beams of light ignited, and the stage was flawless. There was one individual standing center stage with profound words coming straight from the heart. Bold. Beautiful. Speaking directly to my heart. He was making declarations over the event. But not just over the event. Not just over the city. Not even just over our nation. He was speaking over the entire earth! And he meant what he was saying.

With a response from the crowd agreeing with his declaration, the music took off and the entire colosseum, filled with more than twenty thousand individuals, stood up and sang unto the Lord. It was a circumference of oneness. I couldn't even hear my own voice. And let me tell you, I could clear out a congregation in any church with one note. This, I knew, was something special.

It was Passion 2014, led by Louie Giglio and special musicians such as Chris Tomlin, Kary Jobe, and David Crowder, along with influential speakers Francis Chan, Christine Cane, and John Piper. Each one poured themselves out on stage and pointed to one individual—Jesus Christ. It was my first time ever attending a conference—especially one like this. I didn't know what to expect. Sure, I assumed it was going to be another church event that would inspire me and make me feel good about myself. But I felt this time would be much different. I came in with the intent that I was going to break through something, not just attend an influential gathering. I was going to find my purpose, dig deep, and release it for the world to have because what I had, the world needed. I just knew it. But if I were going to find this gift, I needed to go to the Gift-maker, who was in this place. And it wasn't going to be just given to me—I had to search for it. Deeply.

If you are reading these words and they are specifically speaking to your heart, there is a good chance this book was not just placed into your life by coincidence. There is a resource behind the curtain ready to reveal some things to you. You may not know where you are going, but you're ready. You may have some questions along the journey, but the destination is within sight. There may be a stirring in your heart that says, *I know I have purpose.* You just haven't identified it yet. There is a reason you have been given life. Sure, life has its ups and downs, but there is more to the equation than just going through the motions.

The story written above was my first experience as a believer, and it showed me a different side of the coin. I had viewed life through the lens of a different scope for far too long, and now I was witnessing something grander. I was literally witnessing heaven here on earth! Everyone's story has a beginning. Some stories begin after a tragic accident. Others begin with a divine encounter. But something happens when our minds shift and we decide to go after greatness. You, my friend, have greatness instilled deep within your soul, and this greatness is begging to come out.

This is going to be a new path for you. A journey never witnessed before. Many people have one thing that changes everything about their lives. I'm hoping this book is just that! Inside this God-given book you are going to witness supernatural testimonies of ways God's hand strategically swiped over my life. Not your typical social media news feed swipe, I'm talking the fatherly hand of God resting His palm on my soul.

There will be jaw-dropping encounters between individuals and God, just like you have viewed in the Bible. There will be movements that cannot be overlooked. And there will be inspiration to show you how God can effectively move in your life just as much! In addition to the testimonies, practical teachings along the way can help you to find your purpose, and they include marching orders to take what you have learned, build up knowledge, and apply it to your life. My purpose is to give you purpose, so come hungry—you are about to ignite a flame you never knew existed. To start, we are going to begin with you.

Preload and Output

I want you to imagine, for just a second, a factory filled with products all purchased, labeled, and sitting on the shelves. Each one of these packages has a specific destination. They are all different yet created by the same manufacturer. Some took time to build, while others were easy to assemble. The manufacturer took precise measurements, thought critically about the products, and assembled these priceless items.

Go big.

Think of a company that has unending space. Let's choose Amazon. I'm not sure if you're aware of this, but Amazon has a warehouse that is more than 1 million square feet in size. It is known as "Earth's biggest selection." That's unthinkable! It is housed with online retail, computer services, consumer electronics, digital content, and the like. It shows us wide diversity all coming from one manufacturer—yet still, all going out in different directions.

This here is an illustration of heaven. All the packages— you and I—are ideally made by one Creator, God. He specifically designed each one of us for a purpose. "Before I formed you in the womb I knew you; Before you were born I sanctified you; I ordained you a prophet to the nations" (Jeremiah 1:5). God, in all His splendor, made you precisely the way you are. Even before you knew you had life, He was well aware of your soul. He gripped you like a father holds his child. And then, in the right moment, He brought you here to the earth—not just to live, but to live abundantly!

We have to take into consideration the thought of knowing that He gave us life to live out according to His purpose. If not, we struggle with this understanding and fall into an identity crisis, losing ourselves in the process. We need to begin this part of the journey by inventorying ourselves and what makes us—*us*. If we want to delve into the core of who we are, we must first search the heart.

The heart is the single most important organ of the body and the main reason you are alive right now. Can you feel it? Lub-dub, lub-dub. The vascular system attached to the heart would be approximately 60,000 miles long if unraveled and laid single file. That's unfathomable! Some specialists say the heart is where the soul resides. I would have to agree— everything that flows from your life is accompanied by the heart. If we are to ever understand who we are, we must first understand how this life-giving organ functions.

The heart consists of four chambers along with vessels, arteries, and muscle fibers conjoined to make up this miraculous instrument. It ejects recirculated blood from the incoming organs and extremities and sends oxygenated blood back to the body. Cardiac output is the amount of blood the heart pumps in one minute. Sorry, medical geek here. Every process and every calculation of output are dependent on the heart rate, contractility, preload, and afterload. Preload is the amount of stretch the heart has prior to ejection. If at any time the preload is altered or does not meet suitable criteria, the heart does not eject the amount of blood needed for the body. And it fails.

Your life is dependent upon preload and output. Preload, the amount of intake you receive, will dictate the amount of detail your life will give. Think of preload as anything that you intake through your vision, your hearing, and your environment. If I were to look at unclean things, my output would resemble the same. I would become what I preload into my life. Even the Bible states, "The lamp of the body is the eye. If therefore your eye is good, your whole body will be full of light. But if your eye is bad, your whole body will be full of darkness, how great *is* that darkness!" (Matthew 6:22–23).

I love to listen to worship music—strictly intimate worship that correlates my love to the Father. I get lost in the output of what these worship teams are pouring out of their souls and into my living room, car, or headset. Just listening through my speakers, my spirit seems to feel uplifted because what I am intaking (preload) is ultimately giving me a positive outcome (output). If I were to start listening to death metal, I soon would become angry and my thoughts would begin to race. If you're a death metal addict, more power to you. Some people like that kind of thing. But for me, I need positive preload to provide influential outcomes.

You may need it, too. Start by inserting positive music into your daily routine. It doesn't necessarily have to be worship music. It can be anything that gets your brain to be active and in a good mood. If you are wanting to burn and reach optimal purpose, you need to create a platform of positive preload with positive outcomes.

I spend a majority of my private life listening, watching, and reading influential messages that highlight my preload so that my output mimics what my internal being is receiving. Can I let you in on a little secret? I sing the worst when no one is watching. But it expresses my heart toward God, and here's the formula: it's not how good I am at something, it's how much of myself I pour out to Him—the preload and output of my heart.

In addition to your listening pleasure, what we see and the environment we put ourselves in matters. I recall many years ago, through my reckless living, I put myself into some sticky situations. People around me were not for me, but rather they were for what I represented. What happened over time was that they were sucking the life right out of me.

As Scripture always reminds, "Do not be deceived: 'Evil company corrupts good habits'" (1 Corinthians 15:33). So, no matter how good I was, the bad company was changing my output. I was going nowhere in life, became stagnant, and was lost without any hope. That was until God encountered me one night and changed my life. We'll talk more about this later.

You may be at a point in your life where you are around some pretty uninhabitable environments. These environments can alter your lifestyle and suck you in unknowingly. You may not see it at first, but the people you are around are sucking you dry and leaving you lifeless. But there is always room for change. And change you must if you want to burn like never before. Start putting yourself around other motivational people who are for you. These people should be just as motivated as you are to reach limitless possibilities. It won't be easy at first. The old friends will want to hang on because you had given them a reason to be complacent. Complacency is poor preload. Your output on life will be altered with the spirit of complacency. Instead, be a catalyst who breaks the barrier of impossibility because you were made to shift culture and reach further than your own understanding. Begin by changing your environment, what you listen to, and what you are viewing.

Preload, just like the heart, is a vital component to functioning properly. Today, start stepping out of negative environments and begin finding people who inspire you. Even reach out to people who you see doing things in life and invite them to coffee. Everybody loves coffee. But nobody loves a hopeless life where you feel like you are going nowhere. The more you tap into positive preload, the more you will see your life change. And ultimately, you will have greater outputs that produce more abundant outcomes. Remember, positive preload produces greater outcomes!

Four Chambers

Since we are illustrating with the heart, there is no way we can't cover the four chambers. They are the vital components to our lives. These chambers are distinct to the characteristics of your existence. They are the actuality of who you are and what you know about yourself. For instance, the four chambers that describe my life are: compassionate, opportunistic, passionate, and empathetic. You could even break it down into an acronym for fun: *C.O.P.E.* I'm really good at coping, so it just fits. In these four characteristics of what makes me, I must be able to identify them in my life. I work in the medical field. I know that compassion, passion, and empathy are all encompassed into practicing medicine. Therefore, I know that three of my chambers are functioning at their capacity already. Opportunistic is quality, without a doubt, that is constantly revealed in my life. I am always looking for more ways to advance my life. After all, you only get one. And I find opportunity all the time, or maybe it always finds me?

So, what are your four chambers? What makes you— *you*? Define four characteristics that resemble you. If you have to pause for a moment and put down the book, do it! Don't lose sight of the journey now because we have just begun. These can be anything, such as faithful, insightful, adaptive, and resilient. It doesn't matter what they are. All that matters is that they make up you. Did you think of them?

If we are ever going to find our burn notice, we have to reach the very core of who we are. It's not always easy at first to understand ourselves on a personal level, but it is crucial to our purpose. Now, take those four characteristics and see if you can insert them into your life. Right now. Do they function in your daily walk? If so, great, you have identified the beginning of the journey. If not, don't worry because there is more time to understand who you are and how it can become a part of your life.

The four chambers to your life are equal to the four chambers of the heart (soul). If you are not using each one of your characteristics, then it is likely you are not reaching your full potential. Most of the time people haven't examined the characteristics of themselves or delved deep into the DNA of what makes them tick. I assure you, spend time searching these four chambers and see your identity unfold into miraculous work. Begin by painting your canvas.

Heaven Here on Earth

The wedding invitations had been sent out. The tables were all draped with pristine tablecloths. There was a feast set before the event—ready for the people to indulge. Everyone had been anticipating this big day. The bride and groom were waiting anxiously to marry their loved one— the one whom they cherished the most. The king had sent out an infinite number of invitations to the people of the countryside. Encompassed in this invitation was a group of men. These were not regular men, for they carried something special. They carried what was presumably heaven, and these disciples, who had left everything of their lives, had no idea what they were getting themselves into. Yet.

It was the third day and as the men and women indulged in wine, they ran out. Ouch. As the entire wedding became distraught, "And when they ran out of wine, the mother of Jesus said to Him, 'They have no wine.' Jesus said to her, "Woman, what does your concern have to do with Me? My hour has not yet come" (John 2:3–4). This is Jesus's mother were talking about here. The one who birthed the Messiah and changed His diapers. And He responds with "Woman?" But He wasn't talking from a disrespectful point of view. He was prophesying that His time here on earth, when He would die for everyone, had not come yet.

Shortly after, "His mother said to the servants, 'Whatever He says to you, do *it*'" (John 2:5). Can you picture for a moment the anxiety that filled their thoughts? The anticipation of uncertainty? Like, what was about to happen next? The disciples had come across Jesus, who told them He was going to take them places they'd never been and touch people that could not be touched, and they simply dropped everything and followed Him. They went from listening to Him to now seeing His power put into practice!

Suddenly, Jesus tells the men to fill all the jugs with water. Step back David Copperfield: you're about to eat your lunch! Then, draw out a portion of the water and set it before the king of the wedding. The king looked down and witnessed something that had never been seen before. He was witnessing water being turned into wine! "And he said to him, 'Every man at the beginning sets out the good wine, and when the *guests* have well drunk, then the inferior. You have kept the good wine until now!'" (John 2:10).

This was the first miracle ever performed by Jesus, and He wasn't even impressed—not even a little. What was happening, in all this chaos, was Jesus was showing the manifestation of God to His people. He was literally bringing heaven, in all its glory, here to the earth. And the disciples were getting a piece of it. Sure, they left everything behind, but now they were confirming their decision! And

He was giving them permission to do the same—to bring heaven here to earth.

You have the capability and the capacity to bring heaven here to earth. Imagine that Jesus's mother is looking at you—directly into your eyes—and confidently states, "Do everything He says!" You, not knowing the outcome, just begin to believe and see the results of your obedience. You stepped out in faith, and in return, God showed you His power!

Maybe you have felt a passion in a certain area. Maybe you have struggled with not following through. But God isn't looking for people who are capable on their own. He is more reliant on people who follow His instructions that make them capable. You don't have to be able—all you have to do is be *available*. Trust Him in every area, every decision, and every desire that who He says He is will get you to your destination. The disciples had no clue what the future held, but they believed Jesus was who He said He was. And miraculously the journey of heaven began.

Notice how the king emphasized, "You saved the best for *last*." The thing about heaven is that God does not give to the first, but He saves the best for last. He looks for people who are inferior, or without, who are in need, and more than anything, that one lost soul. "So the last will be first, and the first will last. For many are called, but few chosen" (Matthew 20:16). Jesus gave a particular parable about that one lost sheep. "What man of you, having a hundred sheep, if he loses one of them, does not leave the ninety-nine in the wilderness, and go after the one which is lost sheep until he finds it?" (Luke 15:4). Now, this seems like a weird story, I get it. But you have to understand the significance.

God is looking for that one lost person. Sure, He still cares for the ninety-nine other sheep, but it's that *one* lost that He desires the most. "For God did not send His Son into the world to condemn the world, but in order that the world through Him might be saved" (John 3:17). So, you see, heaven wants everyone, *everywhere.*

Imagine heaven as a lighthouse, constantly panning across the ocean of life looking to protect and shine. It is a navigational system, aiding to warn people of dangerous areas and direct traffic at sea. The first are never first in the kingdom. They are always last. This may appear as a buzz kill if you are wanting everything first. Ironically, it's the last that will be *first.*

In order to find our burn notice, we must first become humble in the process. We need to let go of ourselves and stop putting ourselves first. "But He gives more grace. Therefore He says, 'God resists the proud, But gives grace to the humble'" (James 4:6). Instead, look for ways to uplift others around you. Start by praising people for their promotions, even though you feel like you deserved it. If someone is a blessing, send them a message about how inspired you are by his or her life. If a family member is struggling, step in and see how you can help. Humility is higher than you think! It has the ability to give you strength and power. The world believes that everyone should work to get their own. "That if you're not first, you're last" as

Rickie Bobbie would say from *Talladega Nights*. But it's actually dead last that reaps the reward.

There will be instances in your walk with God where you have the ability to bring heaven here to earth. Don't be thrown off course by distraction. Interruptions will happen, and you have to be able to identify them as they come along. There are divine appointments set up for you to help people along their paths where you can be a kingdom-changer, ultimately, showing God to His people. Let me show you.

Heaven in the Hospital

A buddy and I were heading to the hospital to give encouraging words to a man who had been admitted to the psych facility. As we approached the doors, there were some staff members behind the desk who pointed us down the hallway where we believed the entrance was. As we made our way down the hallway, we approached the entrance to the locked-down facility. I hit the button.

"Can I help you?" said a loud voice over the intercom. "Yes, we're here to see John," I responded. "There's no one here by that name," the voice said. *That's strange. This is where they said he'd be.* We had found out it was the wrong side of the hospital. Then, suddenly, a voice shouted, "Aaron, Aaron!" I turned around, and it was an old coworker, Paula, who I used to work with. She was so full of smiles and bliss. Then God dropped it on my heart to ask a question she needed answered. "How's life?" I asked. She stopped dead in her tracks, and her grimace turned to gloom.

Her eyes filed up with tears, and she responded, "Not good." She began to open up and tell me how her family had been in a crisis. We are talking a family-filled household of hopelessness. You could tell she was completely surrounded by darkness. My buddy and I reached over to her and prayed diligently—right there in the middle of the empty hallway.

Tears hit the floor as if there was a complete downpour inside the building. But we knew these were not tears of sadness. These were tears of hope. God was peeling away all brokenness and restoring life back into this mother. Afterward, we asked if she had a home church she attended. "To tell you the truth, it has been forever since I have been to church," she said. We encouraged her to get involved in a local church, one that would support her. By the time we parted ways, you could see the shift in the mood. It felt literally like heaven had cascaded all across the walls.

As we made our way back to the clerks behind the desk, they were gone! They had completely vanished. We looked at each other, with laughter instilled, knowing that what just happened was not a coincidence but a God-given, divine appointment. We knew that our Father wanted us to not only encourage one lost sheep in the psych facility but also another who was just down the hallway. Think about it.

We were there for one hopeless individual. And God wanted to throw us off course, an interruption if you will, so that we could go after another soul that needed to be touched as well. She needed an encounter with heaven. And God needed His workers to bring the good news. Two realms completely colliding together for one purpose—hope. This is what Jesus means by that one lost sheep.

What if you could be that person who engages another lost soul? Would you obey? Would you let go of your emotions? This is the difficult part. Letting go of your uncertainty and just listening to what God is saying. He is speaking all the time.

In the end, we found the right doors and brought encouraging words to a man who also was hopeless. The situation brought not only more faith to others around us, but it also brought more faith to us! This is what it means to carry heaven and shift culture. Let us walk around daily and breathe life into other people. It is your destiny to show the way for others—ultimately, igniting a fire deep within your soul. Your pilot light will no longer just dimly burn. Your pilot will explode with faith you never knew you had before.

This is the first of many chapters that will not only instruct you by giving practical teachings, but through personal testimonies it will inspire you to do more and to go farther than you have ever imagined. God is the God of infinite possibilities. Remember, you have the ability to manifest heaven here on earth. Whatever you intake (preload) will produce the outcome (output). Make sure you do it humbly and not for yourself. Because your gift is not for you, it is for *others* to enjoy! So, let's ignite a flame. Let's see how big your fire can get. Everything has a beginning. Come prepared because the next chapter is an eye-opener. Let me show you what happens when you begin a movement.

Marching Orders

I want you to dedicate one week to prayer. Start by reading one chapter per day and utilize free time to pray. Find a quiet spot. It may be your living room, your car, or a local coffee shop, but wherever it is, go there daily and read. Allow the Word of God to transform you. Pray this: *God I know I have purpose. Show me my purpose. Use me to reach people around me, and improve my relationship with you.* Pray this every day for one week. Journal your thoughts if you have to. He is always speaking. We are preparing your spirit to receive revelation from God. And it's profound! Be ready. Your life is about to change for the better, and God is going to show you your burn notice. Good luck!

CHAPTER 2:

The Beginning of a Movement

t was September 2012, and my head was completely submerged under the water. Held down by two pairs of hands, my eyes were open underneath the body of water. I had never been in this predicament before. Let's be honest, looking back at the entirety of my life until this point, there was no way—come Hades or high water—I should be where I was. And then in what seemed like forever, I was released and came up out of the abyss. As I looked across the horizon, there were shouts and encouragement that would have destroyed a subwoofer competition. I looked to my right only to be hugged by my suspect, and again, hugged by the other person to my left.

I had finally done it. Through the most impossible situation known to man, I was baptized. The hands that held me down were a pastor and his assistant. The loud screams and hand claps were given by the congregation in the parking lot. And it couldn't have happened on any sunnier day.

I believe this day was specifically siphoned out for me. It was "Aaron's Day." Written down in the Book of Life, this day should be celebrated every year like I celebrate my first birthday. While I had experienced many birthdays before, this day commemorated my rebirth. Don't worry, I didn't have to go back into my mother's womb like Nicodemus in the Bible thought. He still to this day can't figure it out since it is a mystery to all mankind.

Everything in life has a beginning. Sometimes it's the birth of a new child. Other times, it's the beginning of a new career. But whatever the beginning is, it has to start somewhere. You see, people believe that life is complete at the resurrection. But might I add something to the mix of our equation? Life begins *after* the resurrection.

When we die to ourselves, that's when life begins! Historically, men and women have tried to figure everything out on their own. Through personal experience and human knowledge, they have accumulated their proverbial responses to what or why they believe what they do. What they soon realized is that they struggle with the fact of finding themselves and acknowledging their own identities. They wonder who they really are, why they are really alive, and for what purpose. If we were ever to get to the true meaning and purpose of our lives, we would have to give up what we want the most—control.

Finding a Fit

When I was a young boy, I went to a Methodist church. It was a small church compromised of closely-knit family and friends. With no more than forty people in attendance, we sang hymns together, accompanied by an old-fashioned organ. I can recall the sound of the pipes playing. I wasn't interested in what happened at church as a boy. I attempted to find my place in many other things, such as popularity, social groups, and culture.

Now that I had come up out of the waters, as a new creation, I wanted to find my *new* fit. I came to church because I knew that was where you went to find God. So, after I had fully given my life to Him, I began saying a prayer that would be chanted for weeks to come, "God, help me to find my fit."

Have you ever chanted a prayer like this before or any particular prayer that would echo into eternity? Sometimes we pray but do not receive an immediate result or the answer we particularly desire. I've been there, but I was diligent with this prayer and knew my answer would come if I would continue believing it would happen.

I don't know if I told you this or not, but I was an avid church hopper. I don't even know if they can categorize that title, but it described me. I was constantly looking for the church where I wanted to grow. I would attend one early service in the morning and then race to the next church just in time to sit down and hear the next opening song. I ran across thousands of people, met many outgoing greeters, and was prayed over by many members in different settings. I didn't know what I wanted—I just knew that I wanted more of God.

Then, one day, I was hanging out with a group of young adults at the church. I had been exploring the different small groups, but on this particular Sunday, I was asked to speak with the leaders of this young adult ministry. They had shut the door behind me and sat directly in front of me.

"How are you?" the leaders asked me.

"Great! Just excited to be here," I replied.

"We have noticed how much you have been coming." They continued. "We want to give you an opportunity to become a leader with this young adult ministry. What do you say?"

I sat and pondered for a second as if I didn't really hear what was coming out. I wasn't there for a title. I wasn't there to be recognized by others. I was simply there because I loved God and loved people. That was it. And here I sat, listening to these words come from their mouths, and the words implied to me, "You *fit* here!"

I took the job as a young adult leader and got plugged into this specific church. And the characteristics and experience I would receive while at this ministry would be the foundation to what was to come. After all, I knew I was on the right path to life. Right? Oh, how things would change, and my life would majorly shift in a new direction.

The Voice

I was deep into the young adult ministry and my relationship with God couldn't have been any better. I did the ritualistic things that churchgoers are supposed to do. I attended church every Sunday. Read my Bible like a good little follower was taught to do. I even attended extracurricular events, such as life groups, after-hour restaurant gatherings, and your once-in-awhile group messages between believers on Facebook. I was what you would consider a "cookie-cutter Christian." But what I was in for was a whole different meaning to church, and it would come when I least expected it.

The church doors had opened, and I was in my usual check-in-early-and-greet-people-at-the-door mode. My smiling face, I could tell, was impacting people as they entered through the door. With their firm handshakes and kind gestures back, they were feeling the love of God. The crowd was ready for their next experience as they took their seats anxiously for the lights, glitz, and glamor. The stage was set. The worship band was well prepped. And with a sudden boost of sound, everything fell into motion as the entire colosseum went into worship.

My hands lifted to the sky, and my mouth opened wide as I was singing unto the Lord. I was completely abandoned— sold out. I knew and felt God with every wavering tug. Then suddenly, I heard something.

"Get outside these four walls!" The voice thundered.

I stopped immediately and opened my eyes as if someone was in my face making this statement.

Nothing.

I looked behind my right and left shoulders, and all I could see were other worshippers, paying no attention to what I was doing while being in their own element.

I suddenly became uncomfortable because either someone was messing with me, provoking me to leave the church, or the devil was out to get me! Putting what I heard off, I continued to fall back into worship.

There was nothing that changed the rest of that day, but what I heard was a mysterious voice with no resonant connection that made any sense. *Why would someone want me to leave the church? Did somebody not care for me? Or was the devil attempting to persuade me to leave the church?* There were definitely some discomfort and questions I was having, but my life went on that week—just like any other week, doing the same things over and over.

That next Sunday it was the same rituals. Get up. Say my morning prayers. Get a little pre-gaming chapter of the Bible in before church, and off I went! Nothing was different. The people were all in their same, instinctive seats. The worship team gathered at the stage. Everyone anticipated the lights, and off we went.

I fell back into my same, every Sunday, church mode. Worshipping and praying. Then suddenly, again it happened.

"Aaron, I need you outside these walls!" the voice thundered.

What is going on! Am I losing my mind? Where is that noise coming from? This same voice kept going. Sunday after Sunday, it kept getting louder, making me more uncomfortable. After church I was begging my wife to pray for me as I thought I was losing it! She, being the great wife that she is, prayed fervently for me every week. But every time I stepped foot in those doors at church it would hit me like a rushing wind. I was now to a point that I couldn't sit at church but had to pace back and forth consistently. People probably thought that I either had a bad bladder infection or I was sitting on coals from all the sin I had produced over the week. Thank God, no one asked me what was going on. Maybe they should have? Or maybe there was a reason for this mystical voice?

Something about the Streets

My phone had rung. It was Jeff, a good buddy of mine who earlier in the year had told me that we were supposed to get together for some profound reason.

"Aaron, I think we are supposed to go feed people in the streets?" Jeff said softly.

As I heard his voice through the phone, my heart began to race. What he was saying seemed to have somehow reached my soul, and I reacted.

"Yes!" I shouted without hesitance. "That's what we need to do!"

"Okay, I'll be over to your house in a minute." Jeff said.

I put the phone down and ran to my wife. "Honey, I think we are supposed to go feed the people in the streets," I said.

She immediately looked over at me and nodded as if to confirm her yes. She always knew I was a burst of energy;

so, when I came tumbling in, this wasn't a new occurrence for her. We packed thirty sack lunches full of peanut butter sandwiches, heavily salted chips, and a monster cookie. It was no five-star cuisine, but it would do the trick.

Jeff had arrived.

We had gathered the sack lunches and hit the streets in a four-door, Ford pickup. Now, you and I both know that you can pretty much find every homeless person on a busy four-way intersection almost as frequently as McDonald's restaurants. Right? But there was nobody! Nowhere. Nevertheless, we kept driving for well over an hour with no sign of life. I became increasingly frustrated. "God, I feel like we are meant to give these sack lunches to needy individuals," I prayed.

Then I felt a nudge that told me, "Keep going." We did. Not even twenty minutes later we pulled down an alley, and, unbeknownst to me, there was a group of people directly in front of our vehicle. I looked at my wife and Jeff as if I were going out into a wild pack of lions, "Okay, this is it—the time is now," I said as I got out of the pickup.

There were thirty people in the alley waiting to be fed. I got out the tray of sack lunches, and the people swarmed to me, like a hive of hungry bees. I started handing out food and my wife and Jeff followed. We had also grabbed our old, used coats as some people were out there in the cold with nothing but a tank top. As I began handing out food and coats, I asked if anyone needed prayer for anything, not that I was above them or just because they were homeless but because I felt the Spirit of God fall upon me.

People started asking for prayer, requesting reconciliation for their lost family members and children, praying for jobs, praying for them to get their hope and faith back, and praying for strength to break their addictions. The list kept growing. Then I noticed many disabilities in the crowd. I spoke over that. Deaf ears suddenly opened up. Backs started coming back into alignment. Ankles healed. If your reading this and it's hard to believe, trust me, I was in much awe myself! And then right in the middle of all this, I heard the voice again. "This is what I have called you to!"

Tears started to swell up as I stepped back out of the crowd and saw the Spirit of God flowing through the people and the evidence of things I once had not seen. The whole time that I was in church God was telling me, "Get outside these walls," so that I could pursue my purpose! It was my calling. My dream. Something special. I was at a loss for words, but I knew there was importance behind this movement. So, we continued on, week after week, handing hot cocoa and sandwiches out of the back of our vehicles. There was no structure to it. Basically, whenever we felt the need to go, we would pack up the trunk and leave. As we continued to feed people out of the back of our vehicles, God told us to find a central location to feed and minister to the people in the streets, and we set up in a park near downtown.

If You Love Them, They Will Come

Word began spreading as we continued to gather every Sunday at the park. On the first week, surprisingly, thirty people showed. For the next week, fifty came. Then seventy-five. 100. Before we knew it 200 people were showing up at the park every Sunday, not just to receive a meal but to receive prayer, to fellowship, and to be with people who were dedicated to them. With so many people, families, and friends, who had given up on them in the past, we were the ones to carry their burdens. It became the first church in the streets! *Was I seeing a different side to what resembled church? Was this what God was calling believers to do? To reach the unreachable? Save the unsaved? Church the unchurched? Give and not receive?* Things were definitely perceived from a different point of view for me. I had been so consumed with doing church that I had missed the opportunity of helping those who were in need. I was self-consumed and not outwardly focused.

In order to find your burn notice, you have to begin somewhere. The disciples had left their boats when Jesus said, "Follow Me," not knowing the outcome and, ultimately, walking with the Son of God. David had to make the decision to pick up the stone, place it firmly in his slingshot, and propel it toward Goliath, defeating an entire army with his small stature. Noah, hearing from the voice of God and obeying what He told him, knew that there would be a flood and that God needed him to build an ark. So, he picked up the first board and laid the first nail. In the same manner, you have to start somewhere, too.

When you are in the will of God, it will not appear normal to you at first. Maybe it was a glimpse of something you saw throughout your day. Perhaps it came in a strange dream and, though you can't connect the dots, all you have to do is implement the idea. Mine came in the middle of a church service. Though I had no training or qualifications, God chose me to step outside the walls so that I could build what He wanted to be done. A movement is not moving from one point to another, a movement is taking what the world perceives as unchangeable and completely changing it!

Jesus came, against all odds and religious resistance, and only did what the Father wanted. "For I have not spoken on My own authority; but the Father who sent Me gave Me a command, what I should say and what I should speak" (John 12:49). He did not come to be comfortable in His own lifestyle, but rather He came to shift the earth. If we lead by this example, we will soon see rewards. All God needs is your *yes*, and He will do the *rest*. I'm positive. But what happens along the way is that we see God being active in our lives and we know that He is telling us something, but we respond in fear, not faith, and miss our God-given moment. If we are to accomplish and fulfill our purpose we have to, "Walk by faith, not by sight" (2 Corinthians 5:7).

If you give God an inch, He'll take you ten miles. It's not that you need to be qualified or carry a theology degree. Anyone who is available is accessible in the kingdom of God. And access will be granted to you if you proceed. "Ask, and it will be given to you; seek, and you will find; knock, and the door will be opened to you" (Matthew 7:7). Have you knocked? Have you sought? Have you ever asked? Maybe you have been pushing on a door that says pull? Directly on the other side of the door may be an endless opportunity of blessings and reward just waiting for you. And it's where you can make history! If you actually separate the word "history," you will see that it says *His story*, which is continuing with your life. The Bible did not end with Revelation. On the contrary, the Bible is still continuing with your life! God is writing more stories and miracles with a fine-point pen that is artistically being drawn on the canvas of life.

Begin somewhere. Know if there is no movement, there is no forward motion. So it has to start somewhere. Reach into your bag of endless talents and treasure and mark your place in *His story,* for you are about to leave a legacy for the world to document. And where there is movement, there are miracles.

Do You Believe?

Having church in the streets was no small endeavor, and it was very messy. That's a good word for an unstable environment—*messy*. Having service under a pavilion in the park without any exterior walls drew in some characters. It drew in the needy. It funneled in addictions. Conflict and controversy between other individuals in the congregation became a common thing. Because what we were doing was presenting the kingdom of God, and the devil wanted no part in that equation, so he brought resistance.

Jesus was very compassionate for the lost, the broken, the poor in spirit, and those who were overlooked. He paid good attention to little boys who struggled with epilepsy, casting out that evil spirit. He would stop a funeral assembly while on their way to bury the son and miraculously raise him from the dead. Let's face it, if there was one specific place in Joplin, Missouri, where He would minister, this would be where Jesus would reside.

I started seeing things from a different perspective. Instead of seeing brokenness, loss of identity, and reckless behavior, I was literally seeing the kingdom directly in front of me through the lens of Jesus. More profoundly, I saw people who needed a Savior. This was no patty-cake ministry anymore—we were dealing with people who internally were crying out for help.

Then there was John. John was a middle-aged man who had been coming to our services for months. Always intoxicated. Never sober. At times he would play it up as if he were sick and wrap himself up in a blanket, claiming to be cold. But we all knew that from sunup to sundown he was always drinking. This did not change anything on our parts. I remember a volunteer came up to me one day and asked what we were going to do about the drug and alcohol activity these people were bringing to the service. My response was very nonreligious.

"We love them," I quickly responded.

And she just sat there for a second and responded, "That's good. Let's do that." She then went back to serving.

You see the church has pushed people away for centuries. If I am supposed to represent Christ, how does the world perceive Him through my life? Every week when we encounter these so-called "unchurched" individuals, we do nothing but love, guide, equip, and inspire them to be something they were created to be.

John, however, was a very difficult individual to reach. But one Sunday he showed up and was sitting over at a table all by himself. He had his head submerged in between his arms and was sobbing. After we had served the people their meals, I walked over to John to see what the matter was. He wouldn't raise his head, and all I heard was his crying. The table was soaked by his tears. Again, I asked, "What's going on, John?" He finally opened up.

"I have been having these headaches for the past couple of months," he sobbed. "So, I went to the doctor this week, and he did a CT of my brain." There was a moment of silence. He continued, "They found a tumor on my brain, and the doctor said I only had a year and a half to live."

I could not believe what I was hearing. In front of me was a man with no hope and no direction. And now he really had no future. I called in all the leaders that surrounded me. We gathered like a huddle of players, and I gave them the update on his terminal illness. We locked arms as a team, and we asked John a profound question regarding his situation.

"John, do you believe that God can heal you today?" I asked.

"Yes . . . Yes, I believe," he said.

And then we prayed over his head. We prayed with confidence. And I felt the Spirit of God so thick in the park that you could have cut it with a knife. This man, I believe, was not feeling a religious experience. I believe that he was given an encounter with his Creator.

The next week the crowds kept coming. What I was experiencing was overflow because the need of the people in this community was insurmountable to the resources being given. I heard a shout through the crowds. "Aaron, Aaron!" the voice shouted.

As I looked over to my left, I saw a man approaching my vision. It was John, and he was sober! He had a big, gleaming smile that lit up his face. "I went to the doctor this week for a follow-up appointment," he said. "They found no tumor on my brain! I'm healed!"

He rushed over to give me a hug with new tears of joy on his face. Praise God for His miraculous healing! This was the first of many miracles that started showing up at the park. Every week John kept coming back sober. He was wearing new attire as well. His hair was combed as if he came off a *GQ Magazine*. John's life was forever changed that day. But if it hadn't been for the opportunity that we were giving people, John would more likely still be stuck in his ways and would soon have found himself gone from this world.

I want you to take a moment and just think of how many people you come across daily who are in need of hope. I bet that if you went back and pondered the amount, you would be amazed. You have the ability to change lives all around you. So many people are looking for a podium—a stage where they can be recognized by others and can fuel their motivation from that. But if you don't reach people on an individual level, God will never give you more opportunity on a crowded stage. Jesus always focused on the individual.

Sure, He spoke in front of crowds. But when He was speaking to more people, His messages became more convicting and uneasy to digest. He never forgot about the one lost sheep. Likewise, we should find individuals who are in need of a Savior.

The fire of God lives and is ignited at the very center of you. If things are going to begin, they have to be ignited. A flame is sparked from an external resource. What fuels you? What moves you? What brings you motivation? All it took to begin this movement was an obedient response. Obedience is *your* response to God's voice. "So Samuel said, 'Has the Lord *as* great delight in burnt offerings and sacrifices, As in obeying the voice of the LORD? Behold, to obey is better than sacrifice, *And* to heed than the fat of rams'" (1 Samuel 15:22). You may have sacrificed your time, your talent, and your treasure, but the real question here is are you obedient? Sacrifice is giving up what we *don't* care to keep, and obedience is giving up what we *care* to keep. If God has given you a mind, He has ignited creativity.

The question I asked John, "Do you believe?" is just as important to your life as it was to his. "Now faith is the substance of things hoped for, the evidence of things not seen" (Hebrews 11:1). Though we cannot see the kingdom of God visibly, His presence is invisibly seen. You may have been looking in all the wrong areas. We think God rests on a mountaintop or maybe comes only during a church service. On the contrary, His presence is found in the deepest, darkest places, where hopelessness lurks. For me, I was seeing the kingdom of God in the park, without walls, among hundreds of homeless men, women, and children who were addicted, overlooked, and without. My perspective had shifted from being in a comfortable church setting to now being at an uncomfortable park without walls, agenda, or direction. Where would this movement end up next? Time would only tell.

Marching Orders

Purpose begins somewhere. I love Nike's statement, "Yesterday you said tomorrow," because tomorrow is today. There's no excuse to not start. You have to begin somewhere. Find a fit with a group of motivated people who have the same vision or beliefs as you. There is fuel for your fire when you get into the right environment of like-minded individuals. Maybe you have put off a dream? Have you been procrastinating on a desire? The best advice I can give to you is *don't*. Don't be intimidated. Don't *put off* what God has *put on* your heart. "For as the body without the spirit is dead, so faith without works is dead also" (James 2:26). So, you can believe all you want, but if you don't apply it to your life, it sits, goes nowhere, and becomes stagnant. And nobody likes stale water. The distance God can take you will begin with your best foot forward. So, walk out your calling. Better yet, burn with a beginning! Once you begin never underestimate where God will take you next. Everything in life begins somewhere. And it starts with a very particular word—obedience.

CHAPTER 3:

Love without an Agenda

We as humans are comprised of many different things. Though we appear different appearance-wise, physically, and through a plethora of unique characteristics, there is one language we all speak—love. Love is a funny thing. We use it verbally to announce our compassion for one another. We wield it to exchange words as though to confirm our friendships and close relationships. We even express it through gifting to help capture moments of gratitude and worth for that one special individual. Love even has different languages according to Gary Chapman who outlines five ways to express and experience love: gift giving, quality time, words of affirmation, acts of service, and physical touch.[1] Which one is yours? I'll hold off on telling you mine.

Love is even traditionalized in the exchanging of vows for the day of marriage when you say, "I do." Valentine's Day has become a holiday of love, where you hope to find that one valentine who will share the experience—even if it is for one day. There is even a day that is honored by *The Love Foundation* as the "Global Love Day," where May 1 is a symbolic day of unconditional love, and they call upon all people and all nations to gather together in the wisdom of peace and, you guessed it, love. The definition of love, according to *Webster Dictionary* is a feeling of strong and constant affection for a person.[2] The *Urban Dictionary* has thirty-six different definitions of the word love.[3] Wow!

Though I could probably write another book on love, I'll spare you for now. But what if what love looked like wasn't love at all? What if we were attempting to lure people in with this so-called expression that was not the root of love? What if love wasn't traditionalized, commercialized, scheduled, or routine? What if love had no agenda? Okay, now we're on to something.

The Amazon River

If I were asked by a friend to think of one area on the earth that I would never go, and they pulled out a map, I'm pretty sure I could think of many different areas not to go. You know, places like Russia where the temperature can reach minus 60 degrees Fahrenheit, Ethiopia where the scarcity of food has affected an entire country leading to thousands of deaths a year due to starvation, or Africa where you could get swallowed up by lions just because they think you look like lunch. But if there is one place that I could never go, the first thing that comes to mind is the Amazon River. Yeah, you wouldn't catch me dead there.

The leadership team at my church knew we were supposed to go on a missions trip. Our church had developed great relationships with other sister churches all over the country. But they had also developed a relationship with a church deep in the heart of Manaus, Brazil. Passion & Compassion Ministries led by Aldair and Hiliary Queiroz set up a church and was extending their mission to many different areas all over the country. This was a church we had been pouring into financially, and we had great communication with the leaders there.

So, we sat down with our pastors and prayed about where we should go. And sure enough, God was leading us toward Manaus, Brazil. Great. After communicating with the church down there, they were ready for our arrival. So, we worked. We fundraised and gathered some of our own finances to venture out on this great trip to Brazil. It would be my first missions trip ever. My wife and I were just beginning our relationship with the Lord, and we were open to serving His kingdom.

We had packed our bags and successfully boarded the plane with a group of us open to whatever it was we were supposed to do. But unfortunately, through the process, one of the girls had lost her passport while exchanging flights.

She had looked everywhere, but by the time she noticed it was missing, the flight had already ascended toward its next destination. We had to leave her behind, which was a strike to the body already. We kept pressing and arrived at the city of Manaus, Brazil, where we stayed with a mission's family who had left the United States to become missionaries and live in Brazil. It was hard for me to wrap my mind around an entire family who sold everything and left their jobs in America to pursue a place in Brazil to do God's work. But I admired it! It was what you called true abandonment. It was their burn notice.

Many of the locals had greeted us while we were unpacking. We met a lot of good people who couldn't speak a lick of English. Great! Communication was off, but the love—the love was very apparent. We were fed a meal while at the introductory house and then we headed to the church. The one thing that kept crossing my mind was that it was *hot*! The weather there was muggy. It was above 100 degrees Fahrenheit there with little access to running water, and every time you showered you instantly began to sweat again. Let's be honest, I was miserable.

Passion & Compassion Ministries greeted us as we got off the bus. It was such a sweet welcoming as they greeted us with coffee and crumpets. Nothing was Americanized. I literally had no signal on my phone. I didn't carry a watch. And I knew that the others in my group were feeling the same anxiety. We had no idea what we were getting ourselves into, but we were open to whatever and wherever we were supposed to go because this trip had no agenda!

You may be reading this now and wondering what we were getting ourselves into? Rightfully so, maybe you have experienced a moment in your walk with God where you were uncertain about some things. You maybe had no direction? No instructions? No clue? But you did carry one distinct characteristic—you were open . . . open to whatever God had for your life. You developed a relationship. Or maybe you are currently developing a relationship. Whatever the case may be, you are ready, and you say, "God, here I am to serve you." And then you wait. Good. That is the starting point to what love looks like. It is surrendering your life so that you can have life. It doesn't take a degree, a special quality, or any gift. All God wants is your attention to where He is taking you next.

The trip literally had no agenda. We had no schedule and no sense of time. No service. Nothing. All we had was a group of people who had one thing on their hearts—to love people unconditionally and to listen for God's instructions. So, we set up nights of worship and prayer. We prayed for each other fervently. For the first two nights we bonded relationships and spoke words of knowledge toward each other. It was the setup for what was to come.

After two nights of worship, the pastors got word. They told us they were establishing churches deep in the jungle where poverty was not even a word because their living conditions were below that. Drug activity had run rampant in the jungle. Guns and gang activity were taking over these small villages, and people were losing hope. Families were selling their children to sex traffickers because they felt like they had to do whatever to keep food on the tables for their families—heartbreaking. Running water was nowhere in sight. They had to float miles upstream to the next village to obtain any sort of water supply. Let's put it this way: envision some of the most desolate places in the world, and this could quite possibly be the worst. But this is where the church was invested. And this is where they knew God was up to some big things.

Timbo was a village, hidden deep in the jungle, dedicated to preserving the land by Passion & Compassion Ministries. They had been cultivating this land for some time, and this is the exact destination the church wanted us to minister in. Timbo was located 120 miles away from Manaus, Brazil, and you had to float through the Amazon River to get there. Really? But we came not to set ourselves on our feelings, but we came set on the foundation of our faith! So, we gathered on a boat, and we had no idea where this journey would go next.

You may be open to some things God is wanting to do in your life. And then you are faced with an uncertain challenge. The question here is will you walk through those doors of uncertainty? Often when you do, just on the other side of the door is opportunity—a beginning to the future of your existence and an exploration into a different environment. After all, you were placed on this earth to preserve it and own it. But a majority of the time people get stuck on their feelings and not their faith. I have been there several times. But the Bible instructively tells us, "For we walk by faith, not by sight" (2 Corinthians 5:7).

I found myself in this huge pool of uncertainty. I didn't want to go down the Amazon River, but I did. I wanted to have phone service and get on my phone, but I couldn't. I wanted to know what was going to happen because I was so used to knowing everything, but I didn't. And so here we were, leaving our country, adventuring into Brazil, stepping onto a boat, and floating down the Nile. Off in the distance was a village with no hope. Yet, we were carrying the light of the world in our hearts—enough light to ignite a fire if set in the right area.

We knew we were drawing near the village, and it was dark. We floated for over eight hours to get to our destination upstream through the Amazon River. In the last hour before reaching the village, we assembled together as a family and prayed, "Lord, let your will be done in our lives. We are here to serve you and to reach areas that can't be reached." Then worship broke out. Guitars and voices entered the sky, and people down the Amazon came up out of their half-sunk houses to listen to where the sound was coming from. Curiosity reached their hearts, and they knew the sound was good. It was the preparation before reaching the destination. And suddenly our boat hit land.

It was too dark to get out of the boat, and the village had laid to rest that night. So, we got our hammocks out and slept on the boat. It was large enough for us to sleep and eat, and it provided shelter during our next three days in Timbo. We were hoping to hit this mission running, but for now we rested until dawn. We were exhausted, to be honest. Though we were on fire deep in our hearts, that pilot light would never go out. It only dims for a moment, but eventually, the more you burn the more people around you want what you have.

Morning had come, and we were awakened. Time to get off the boat. We walked up the vast hill only to witness empty hutches all around us. Vegetation was good there, but there was no fruit on the trees. Children were running around with no shoes and looked as though they hadn't washed in days. They were so cute though. The families in these villages all stepped out and glanced as we toured the village. Approximately 400 villagers lived here. Surprisingly, some had smiles on their faces. Maybe it was the fact that they thought we had brought food and water. We approached many different families, not many fathers, and a lot of mothers or women who had taken initiative to be caregivers for the many children. We did get word that a lot of men had fallen into the traps of temptation, so a lot of women and children were left behind.

The women would encourage us to come into their houses and sit. The floors were barely walkable. The stools we sat on were considered luxury to them. The translators helped to communicate for us. Even though they had nothing—food or water, they offered us their hospitality, which was more than enough. Mind blowing. After we went from house to house, separated in different groups, I will never forget the one house that had the aroma of love.

As we approached this out-of-place home. You could tell there was something different about it. The windows had shutters. There was a front porch. It actually had a front door. It was like a mansion set on a hill, centered in the underprivileged village. The woman who owned the house was elderly. She was probably no younger than sixty years of age. And the entire house was filled with children. Their ages ranged from three to sixteen years old. But the inside was immaculate! The walls were painted bright colors. There were televisions in all the rooms. It even had an intact floor to walk on. The kitchen was compulsively itemized and well put together. All the pans, ranging from largest to smallest, were aligned perfectly. She told our tour guide that this was a house of love. Many children were sold into sex trafficking, and this woman had taken the initiative of adopting as many children as possible. Unbelievable.

You could feel the presence of God in this house. I called it "God's House of Love." She told us that God has been the supplier of her and the children's needs, which is why the house was so blessed. No house even compared to this beauty. I had never experienced so much joy in this type of environment. We fellowshipped, had soda, and spoke of God's goodness. It was one of those moments. But as we were exiting her home, we asked if there was anything that we could do for her. She did tell us that she had been having severe lower back pain. We stopped, and we gathered. Certainly, we needed to pray for this woman. So, we laid hands on her back, and she was miraculously healed! She had tears in her eyes and thanked God for our arrival, and we thanked God for her obedience. I even gave her a prophetic word that God was going to bless her even greater and bring more children into her house of love. She accepted the prophetic word as we hugged and exited our fellowship. It was apparent that love lived there.

A Different Kind of Church

Living in Western culture, I have had my fair share of church experiences. I have noticed the supreme transformation where church is quickly becoming an experience rather than an encounter. We are mesmerized by the lights, stage, and show. Overcome by the climax of the ending where all are invited forward as we close with the final song. Everything is scheduled and routine, and if not done correctly, next week we come back and restructure the event. Pragmatism has quickly lured its way into the church system as if we are to perform in a satisfactory working condition. Technologically we become more savvy by making our websites, brochures, and brands more attractive to the viewers. We build brands to help boost the name behind it—ultimately, increasing our numbers and increasing our pockets. But here in Brazil, I did not see this type of church system. In fact, I saw a totally new infrastructure.

Passion & Compassion Ministries was making progress in Timbo. They had dedicated missionaries who were infiltrating the ground and creating good relationships. The village trusted them. With that much trust, they wanted to build a church deep in the heart of the jungle. They began the work and started assembling the structure. What structure you might add? A concrete slab and a frame to keep the roof up. That was it.

This was not your Americanized church. This was a church literally without walls that was deep in the heart of the Amazon, centralized inside the jungle. You couldn't find this church on Google Maps. No, no, this was heaven being brought into an underprivileged area where hopelessness and brokenness were the norm. But God did not send His ambassadors inside the riskiest part of the Amazon to play church. He was wanting the people whom nobody wanted. And that, my friend, is Christ-like!

The group of us were grateful to see such progress and success inside this village. In fact, we were able to engage with the children and women there. During the day they had children's church where they invited every child to come in and receive love. No agenda. No walls. Just love.

Nighttime was quickly arriving, and the missionaries had sat us down as a group and told us about the evening service they had, not just for the villagers but for everyone up and down the Amazon. Tonight, they expected a good turnout as word got out that Americans were in the area, not that we were something special. But to them, we were.

We were to bring the Word of God to the people and share our experiences and wisdom with them. I was more than nervous because I had never been in this predicament before. I was used to a stable church working environment where everyone knew Jesus, but that was not this environment. People were coming to hear what we had to say and to see if truth resonated in our hearts. And the one who would be chosen on our first night in Timbo to present the Word of God would be—you guessed it—*me*.

I couldn't tell if it was the unlivable heat that was drawing sweat from my forehead or the anxiety that consumed my mind. But for whatever it was worth, tonight I knew I would bring my testimony. I would share the distance and the deliverance God gave me in my life.

We got word that some of the biggest drug dealers and traffickers were going to attend church. As if my anxiety wasn't through the roof already, I had to speak in front of all the men who carried darkness with them.

As we approached the wall-less church, we couldn't help but notice that the people inside the church were only women and children. The people outside the church were men. Apparently, church was considered weak and feminist according to the men. So, the brigade of men surrounded the church as if they made the church walls. Weird. But nevertheless, I came with one mission—to bring the Spirit of God and revelation to all who had ears.

The music of worship began to fill the air of the jungle. I could smell the sweet aroma of joy and peace. It was nothing I had ever experienced before. Voices were lifted up and arms swayed in the night life. And then I got my cue. Buzz kill! I had approached the front of the people. With all eyes on me, I blurted my first words, "Greetings from the United States!" *Greetings from the United States? What a nerd!* Those were my first words unfortunately, and they were so cliché and American.

I continued after the embarrassment and gave my testimony. I will spare you the details, but as I was speaking something came over me. It was as if I blacked out. But I just kept moving my mouth.

After the church service closed, something spectacular started happening. The men—both drug dealers and traffickers—came into the church. They started thanking us for our appearance. More than that, they wanted to know more about God and what He was like. They became curious. They became convicted of their behavior. And most certainly they felt a need to change.

Once the people filtered out of the church, we came together as a body of believers and shared testimonies, worshipped, and gave thanks. Something on that concrete slab happened that night. And it was truly an honor to be the hands and feet of God. We got word later that the drug activity in that village had diminished and that families reconsidered selling the children to traffickers. Even drug dealers started leaving the area. Can you believe it?

Can you imagine what it would look like if we did church differently? If we loved people without any agenda? I do. I saw what love looked like to a village of hopeless people. I saw missionaries who weren't after their money, their property, or their land. They were after their hearts. In America we become so accustomed to loving *with* an agenda that we lose the authenticity of the gospel. We have love *with* an agenda. But I believe that once the church begins to manifest the love of the Father, atmospheres and cities will begin to change—much like the church set up in the middle of the jungle. Change happened to a lifeless village. They were being resuscitated by the breath of air these people were giving. My question to you is, "How do we become the church and love people without any agenda?" That's the thing: love has no agenda and, most certainly, love doesn't have any barriers either.

The Red-Light District

As if leaving our country and flying fourteen hours south down to the Amazon River and floating 120 miles upstream into a hopeless village in the middle of the jungle wasn't enough, there was more to our non-agenda-type mission than we thought. We were going to go deeper. Darker. The church had founded a program where they were going out often into the streets to love on prostitutes. You heard it here folks—transgenders, bisexuals, and young women who were selling their bodies for money.

What's even more disturbing is that the government in Manaus, Brazil, enabled these men and women to have a career as an escort. Bringing in thousands of dollars through tourists who financed this type of behavior. You see, in America prostitution is illegal. In Manaus, it's encouraged. So, tourist from all walks of life fly to this predestined area to get their fix and fill the pockets of governmental officials. And the church would be the ones to rescue these sons and daughters from the dark abyss.

Our agenda? Nothing. But to love and acknowledge prostitutes right in the middle of their environment. It's unheard of, I know. We loaded up multiple vehicles and set out for the night. Only a few chosen people were able to venture off while the other half of our group stayed behind and interceded through prayer and worship.

As we drew closer to the red-light district, my heart started to flutter. I was excited and overwhelmed all at the same time. Much of what I was feeling was similar to the experience back at the village just before I gave my testimony. And just as I started having heart palpitations, flashing red and blue lights became the background of our journey.

Closely approaching us were the police, not because we were doing anything wrong, but because we were in the depth of the red-light district. They assumed we were there to purchase product. The government had approved this behavior, but city officials were still trying to bring it down, so they investigated us one-by-one. They didn't speak any English. Luckily, we had our guides who spoke fluent Portuguese. They wanted to know what we were doing, where we came from, and what our intentions were. After much time spent being interrogated, they let us go. That was a close one.

We finally came to our first destination. We had many destinations assigned for the evening. What was our bait to persuade these men and women to talk with us? Soda and cake. Yep! Some missionaries use the Bible, but we used overconsumed corn syrup. Who doesn't love a little carbonation and sugar to open up a conversation?

The group who took us out on this extravaganza had been sowing for months. They had already established relationships with the people in the streets. Surprisingly, these men and women always accepted prayer. They didn't feel like they were in the wrong because the government condoned it. How deceived do you really have to be? Nevertheless, we got the opportunity to pray over them and fellowship right there on the street corner. Shortly after cars pulled up, the girls gladly would exit into their vehicles as they drove off into the night.

Not much was happening. A lot of ingested angel cakes and Dr. Pepper. But we weren't there to put them down or tell them to change their ways. We didn't even preach to them. All we were was an out. A face and a card to let them know if they ever wanted out of this lifestyle that we were an exit—a chance for a better life. Unfortunately, many of them didn't want that. But God had different plans for this night.

We pulled up to our last spot. It was most certainly the deepest, darkest area of the red-light district. Traffic didn't even flow in this direction, and the streetlights were scarce. There was only one female on this corner. I didn't even catch her name. She was short in stature, and her clothes were barely put together. But there was one distinct characteristic that separated her from the other prostitutes—this woman was deaf.

I was chosen to get out of the vehicle with two other female interpreters. We approached the woman as she slowly crept her way toward us. She couldn't hardly even understand the interpreters as she had been deaf since birth. She was very timid. Pointing behind her to signify that her pimp was watching us in the background. Surprisingly, pimps did not see us as a threat. They knew we were there just to talk.

We kept attempting to communicate in some way. We tried sign language, using small, universal gestures to ask her about her life. She lived a rough life. She didn't have much parental support. No education. No friends. No hope.

Then, in an instant, I felt the Spirit of God whisper to me, "Pray, and her ears will be opened." I stopped the girls. I asked them to communicate to the girl and ask if I could pray for her. She agreed. I asked if it would be okay if I laid my hands on her ears. Again, she agreed. So, I instructed the girls to lay hands on her as well.

I placed both of my hands on each ear. *I command, ears be opened! Hearing come back into place. In Jesus's name!* Suddenly, she looked over at me as if I had done something significant. I asked her, "Can you hear me?" As the girls interpreted this to her, she responded with her fingers, "A little."

Then, I heard the voice again, "Pray again, that's not enough." I told the interpreters that we were to pray for her again and that her ears would be opened. They nodded back, and I laid both of my hands over her ears. *Ears be opened, in Jesus's name!*

I brought my hands away from her ears as she drew back and cringed. Physically, you could tell something was happening. She stood back up, and for the first time she was trying to explain to us that she could hear. For the first time in her life she was actually hearing the traffic, sounds, and our voices! I knew this was a chance to tell her who she was.

"Tell her exactly what I am saying," I said to the girls. They nodded.

"You are a child of God," I boldly proclaimed to the girl. "You have purpose."

"You are loved."

You have to understand the significance here. For the first time this woman could hear. And the first words that touched her ear drums were, "You are a child of God." A beautiful, wonderfully made daughter, who is a child of God! This was love. This was love without any agenda because we had no idea what God was going to do on this night. But He had a reason. He had a purpose: that He would use a group of Americans to go deep into the darkest place on the map to find one girl, who was deaf from birth, with no hope, and who would regain her hearing. Wow!

You see love doesn't have to have an agenda. It doesn't even have to know the outcome. All love needs is a voice—a vessel that would say "love wins" and find people who are without hope to receive the love of the Father for the first time. This woman, we heard, still continues to have her hearing intact. And that, my friend, is the continuous love that God wants to give all His children. No matter the sin, lifestyle, or darkness that so easily entraps us. Mind blowing!

The Broadway Bash

The numbers had kept coming in at the park. Week after week we were overwhelmed with the people from all different backgrounds. Everyone had a story. Everyone had pain. Some needed more healing in their hearts than others. Regardless, we had one agenda, which was to continue to love people.

That's a good point here: let love *be* your agenda.

The miracles, signs, and wonders followed. We saw tumors dissolved, joints come back into alignment, and vision restored. I was seeing a different side of the kingdom than I ever had before. And it was life changing! I was so accustomed to regular church, sitting, standing, and listening comfortably in my seat. But that was not the case in the streets here at the park. I was literally on the edge of my seat with every serving hour. I knelt with people who were living at rock bottom. I hugged the foulest-smelling individuals. I prayed for the unthinkable situations. Was I literally in the middle of a battlefield just like Jesus? Was I witnessing exactly what the disciples had encountered during their three years with Him in ministry? Oh, how this environment I found myself in was so unstable, yet there was a profound sense of the Father's presence. Then His voice came again, "You need to have a block party." The voice interrupted the service. Great, here we go again.

I was starting to hear the Father's voice more clearly at this point. I knew it was Him because He was instructing me to do things I never would do on my own. Things like stepping outside the church walls. Yeah, that was a whole new ball game for me. But the more I started obeying and stepping outside of my comfort zone, the deeper and more mysterious my journey would become.

But I still had a lot of questions. *Block party? Where am I supposed to have this? Which area? Neighborhood? And whom should I notify?* You ever have questions begin to pile up in the back of your mind—like you know you heard from God, but you don't even know where to begin? That was me. Luckily, I had established, through serving people in the streets, relationships with other city officials.

The city had been establishing relationships in East Town, an underprivileged area of Joplin where substance abuse, poverty, and gang activity resided. For the past six months, officials had navigated needs in the community, collecting data and statistics about abandoned businesses and underdevelopment. Unfortunately, the neighborhood was a dying community. Businesses had moved out, houses had been abandoned, and hopelessness had rested here. But the city wanted change, so they had a neighborhood meeting. The city heard about what we were doing in the community, so they had cordially invited us to the meeting.

Police, other nonprofits, and hundreds of residents from East Town showed up to the meeting at the Boys and Girls Club. As normal for myself, I showed up fashionably late to meet the other leaders. It was an open discussion meeting that covered the statistics of East Town and ways to improve the community. The residents were angry. They were frustrated because they felt like Joplin did not support this part of the city. Rightly so, it was a dying community with no hope.

After about an hour into the meeting, they asked if anyone had anything to say. It was as if something pushed me to raise my hand, and so I stood up boldly, "Yeah, we want to have a block party." I shouted.

For what seemed like ten minutes, the entire auditorium was silent. You could have heard a pin drop. And the city officials just glanced back at me with that deer-in-the-headlights look, and they responded, "Okay, let's have a block party here in East Town." I finally took a breath as I couldn't believe what I had just said.

After the meeting was adjourned, people came up to us and shook our hands, encouraged by our boldness. We were soon creating a name for ourselves in the community. Great. Because as I was shaking hands with officials, I thought to myself, *How are we even going to pay for this, and who would we gather to see this thing come to life?* It didn't matter. I spoke up and responded to what God was wanting to do in this community. We were going to have a block party.

Word quickly got out we were wanting to have a block party in East Town. We had no clue what we were doing. We thought, *Where were the finances going to come from? Who would we partner up with? What about volunteers? Churches?* All of it! As the questions flooded my mind, my phone began to ring. Churches heard about our passion for the community and wanted to get involved. Money started showing up. People were donating to the cause—and not just frugally. Miracles just kept happening. The news station started promoting it on their stations. Everybody all over the region was so encouraged. But we needed a place to have it. And we knew the prime location over in East Town would be Broadway Street, so we asked the city for them to close it off for the event. But their response was, "No way, no how." Bummer.

Apparently closing down Broadway Street was like shutting down the Golden Gate Bridge. The city utilized the road for emergency responders, and it was nearly impossible to close it off, especially for some random event. So, we waited. And we prayed.

Shortly after, we got a phone call from the Mural Project. There was a building that they had been focused on over in East Town to canvas a side of a building for a mural. The building was located right next to Broadway Street. They heard that we wanted to have a block party, and they wanted to paint a mural. So, we partnered up for the event.

Miraculously, the Mural Project had a good standing with the city, and the city allowed us to shut down a portion of Broadway Street for the event. Unbelievable! So, we set up shop, with Broadway Street partially closed off, and we utilized the other parking lots adjacent to the street for the First Annual Broadway Bash!

Thirteen churches volunteered and set up carnival-type booths with prizes and games. Inflatable bounce houses were centralized for the children to jump in at the event. Radio stations blared music. Donations came from all over to pay for the food. Bubbles filled the air with joy. It was an entirely free event, programmed to love people with no agenda, at no cost!

One-thousand people from East Town showed up to the Broadway Bash. Never had any of these children and parents received this type of generosity before. Overwhelmed with the picture I was seeing, I was able to see the manifestation of the Father among His people. It didn't have to be super spiritual—all it looked like was love. Love was seen through the children's smiles. Love was witnessed through the satisfaction of parents. Love was being manifested by hope through the people. Honestly, I was seeing the harvest of what we had sown into. Hearing God's voice say, "You need to have a block party." Obeying. Not knowing how it would go. Then, everything started to fall into place. And witnessing an entire community that was once hopeless, glancing through the crack, and seeing hope for the first time. That was love.

Impossibility is a common word man likes to use. "But Jesus looked at *them* and said to them, 'With men this is impossible, but with God all things are possible'" (Matthew 19:26). Take, for instance, an entire community with no hope and a leadership crew with no qualifications, colliding together and sharing this experience. It was as if Jesus were fellowshipping with His bride. What appeared impossible for so many was now becoming possible. It was not just giving people hope but fueling a leadership team with faith.

While we were there, the people had approached us and asked, "Did you know that the Washington Education Center is up for sale? You should place a bid on that school."

I thought it was a very peculiar response. *What would we need with a building? An entire school? That's just crazy!* I brushed it off like I didn't hear the statement and continued to love people. The night came to a close, and we were all exhausted. We served 1,000 meals that day. It was a day that would resonate in our hearts forever and be stamped in our minds. We did what appeared to be impossible. Through love the Father came to encounter His children in an abandoned area with no hope and gave them a glimpse of what hope might look like. We were sowing on good ground. We were there for a purpose. That's the thing, if you want to find your burn notice, you must begin to sow good seed.

Marching Orders

Though we are driven by our agendas, schedules, and routines, we need to try something different: try loving people without any strings attached. If you have noticed throughout this chapter, love is a very powerful tool. It can change a community, give hope to the hopeless, and ultimately, let people see God through your daily living. "Let your light so shine before men, that they may see your good works and glorify your Father in heaven" (Matthew 5:16). Try small increments of love in the most absent areas where people don't expect it. You will find that love really has no agenda and that with God there are no limitations attached to that love.

CHAPTER 4:

Seed Sowers

hate gardening. I don't think you heard me clearly: I cringe at the fact that I have to bend over consistently, dirtying my knees, digging my fingers deep within the soil, and planting a seed that doesn't even resemble a plant. More than all that, I don't get the instant gratification of seeing that seed become a living plant. It's not my fault that I don't like gardening. I don't think it was a part of my nature from the very beginning. I always had that gardening-is-for-others-with-a-green-thumb mentality.

My father, on the other hand, is a greenhouse guru. He has strategically studied and developed an entire Eden from the ground up. His home is like the second foundation under his garden. You could probably even make a redneck joke that states, "You might be a redneck if your garden is bigger than your home." Jeff Foxworthy would be so proud. Not only does my dad have an immaculate garden, but he has a water system and can even genetically modify his crops. Overachiever.

I, on the other hand, am lucky if I can even identify a weed in my yard. I'm like picking up good grass only to turn around to what appears to look like a gofer has invaded my territory. I'm pretty sure that I don't even own a pair of gardening gloves, if I were to decide to take up a gardener's lifestyle.

Though you would never see me bent over planting tulips with Martha Stewart nor see me picking through the Missouri Botanical Gardens in St. Louis, there is one very distinct area where I do love planting. And that is planting seeds within *people*.

Much of what we have covered in the beginning chapters has been very inspirational and influencing. We have learned what it means for heaven to reside here on earth, that everything has a beginning, and that the time is *now* for us to burn with passion. Most certainly we can't burn without love. All the more, love without any agenda, understanding how love can influence a community and bring about hope. And now we are going to move toward sowing seeds in our lives. Good seed. Seed that has deep roots and has the ability to take what was planted in our hearts and see that passion develop and blossom into a harvest. We are going to switch gears and move into a genre of practical teaching.

Before we have the ability to change the world around us, we must first have seed planted with us. And by seed, I mean the Word of God. "Another parable He put forth to them, saying: 'The Kingdom of heaven is like a mustard seed, which a man took and sowed in his field'" (Matthew 13:31). Our own fields are our hearts. And the gardens in which these seeds are planted are our lives. So, let's delve into where the initial seeds must be placed. This first seed is the foundational seed.

The Foundational Seed

Before you can even attempt to plant seeds in people, you must first identify the seed planted in you. This is the initial seed, the primary seed—the Word of God, which is alive and active. "All Scripture *is* given by inspiration of God, and *is* profitable for doctrine, for reproof, for correction, for instruction in righteousness, that the man of God may be complete, thoroughly equipped for every good work" (2 Timothy 3:16–17).

In the beginning God made the light, the waters, the earth, the creatures within it, and finally He made man. Not only did He make man, but He made man in His *image*! Grip that reality for one second. God, who owns the stars and continuously canvases galaxies that can't even be viewed with a scope, desired to make man—you—in His image. That is unfathomable!

So, the Lord made a garden and listen to what He did. "The LORD God planted a garden eastward in Eden, and there He put the man whom He had formed" (Genesis 2:8). So not only did He create man in His image, He placed man in His garden. It was God's initial seed.

Now during this time Adam and Eve, who He brought along later so that man wouldn't be alone, were able to have communion with God. They literally walked, talked, and fellowshipped with their Creator. Can you imagine for one second, God, who designed and crafted all of existence, walking up and down the garden, exchanging thoughts daily, probably joking with one another, being by your side? I can't. But Adam and Eve did that. They were inseparable!

The initial seed planted in the garden was placed by God. He knew that man was fit for the job. He actually took pleasure at placing man in His garden and giving Him ownership over every walking and breathing thing. Then, man knew the revelation of God and this inspired Him to continue the work laid before Him. Man delightfully owned what was given to him. He had a sudden passion that was indescribable. It was Adam's first burn notice!

Take Adam's life for example. A man, who was placed in a specific place for a specific reason, suddenly felt passion to push forward with whatever task God gave to him. This is the primitive example we should follow as Christians. Every one of us was born in a specific region for a specific purpose. The Bible says, "For we are His workmanship, created in Jesus Christ for good works, which God prepared beforehand that we should walk in them" (Ephesians 2:10).

Wherever you are today is *exactly* the garden He wants you in now. Sure, there may be times when we move to other locations, but where you are now is where He needs you to flourish.

But the Word of God must be planted in your heart first. Without the revelation of His Word being the navigational system to your life, there will surely be roadblocks along the way. If you learn to submit your life to Him, He will certainly finish the good work that He started when you were born.

Jesus said, "And He who sent Me is with Me, The Father has not left me alone, for I always do those things that please Him" (John 8:29). Jesus knew what it was like to be a Son. No matter whom He spoke to or whose physical nature He miraculously changed, He always did what the Father desired. He was obedient to the Father's voice. Likewise, when the Word of God is planted inside you, suddenly you are able to understand and obey the direction He wants to take you. The foundational seed is the most important seed. And the garden we are currently in is the right location. So, we have to ask ourselves this: are we listening to what God wants us to do, and are we impacting the world around us?

Listening to God's voice isn't always easy, but it is imperative. Adam had no problem understanding the vocal cords of God. He was literally an arm's length reach away. But we forget the fact that God didn't distance Himself from man after the garden. In fact, He brought us closer. And He would use His most decisive formula ever invented—He would use His Son, Jesus, to draw us back in!

When Jesus was merely twelve years old, He did something His parents never thought He would do—He got lost doing His Father's work. Picture, if you will, a boy who wasn't even a teenager yet, sitting in the synagogues with the most theological rulers. He scurried out from under His parents' care while visiting Jerusalem. How rebellious! While His parents were franticly searching for Jesus for three days, they stumbled upon Him in the temple courts, listening to the teachers there. "So when they saw Him, they were amazed; and His mother said to Him, 'Son why have you done this to us? Your father and I have sought You anxiously.' And He said to them, 'Why did you seek Me? Did you know that I must be about My Father's business?'" (Luke 2:48–49).

Can you imagine your twelve-year-old responding to you like this?

There is something significant when you start living your life about your Father's business and not your own. Sure, we have our jobs, our families, our retirement, our lives. But God has called us to a higher standard. He wants us to be about *His business*. This is no three-piece suit showing up at 9 o'clock in the morning and going about your daily business. This is a lifestyle of miraculous signs and wonders that can only be accomplished when doing God's business.

What if the seed that was planted in you had such growth that people around you couldn't help but be attached? Even if it is a small seed at first. "Though it is the smallest of all seeds, but when it has grown it is the largest of garden plants and becomes a tree, so that the birds of the air find shelter in its branches" (Matthew 13:32). Understanding the significance of a little seed—a little faith—in God and what He says will eventually catapult you into an ambience of greatness. Eventually people will want to come and perch on your branches.

This is where we go from the seed being planted in us toward planting seeds in others. God has equipped you with the right seed to reach the right people and to see righteousness be revealed. And it is contagious. People will begin to see genuineness and want what you have. Your passion will transfer into a burning desire to take what you have and give it to the world.

You have the right credentials to sow good seed into people who have dying roots. After all, the gospel was not meant for us to squander and keep, it was meant for us to give it to others. Being a seed sower starts by planting the Word of God into your heart. We must begin every journey with a foundation, and that foundation is taking the Scriptures and making them come alive—alive to the point where we begin to find our burn notice that flames out to others, igniting more relevance of who God is and taking our natural habitat to new levels. It is time we start sowing seeds into the people around us. Let's scatter and then gather!

Sowing Our Seed

So, we understand that the Word of God being initially planted in our lives is imperative to growing good seed. Without it, we won't have the energy nor the direction to find new ways to scatter seed. Being fruitful is a part of being a Christian. Imagine if you grew such large fruit in your life that people couldn't help but come along and pick from your branches? Likewise, the seed sown deep into your heart is never meant for you to keep and hoard. It's meant to be released to others around you.

Let's go back to the passage, shall we? "Another parable He put forth to them, saying: The kingdom of heaven is like a mustard seed, which a man took and sowed in his field, which indeed is the least of all the seeds; but when it is grown it is greater than the herbs and becomes a tree, so that the birds of the air come and nest in its branches" (Matthew 13:31–32). Initially, when you begin your journey with God, it may not appear like much at first. All you had was a desire to seek His face, and then miraculously things started happening. You start to notice growth in your life, and this growth subsequently has no alternative but to reach people around you, people close to you, and people within your sphere of daily living like your neighbors and family. The list is endless.

Ask yourself: Are people wanting what you have? Are you seeing people drawn to you? Are you bearing good fruit? Do people come to you for support? Do they come to you for prayer? Are they seeking guidance from you? These are all valuable questions that should be searched within yourself. Because if you are sowing good seed in your own life, that seed has no choice but to be fruitful and multiply to others. This is where you can identify a part of your burn notice, fanning your flame onto others. Let me show you what seed sowing looks like.

A Place Known for Death

God will plant you in specific gardens for a specific time period. For me, He placed me in a garden while I was finishing my master's program. I was hired on to work at a long-term, acute-care hospital. If you don't know what that is, it is a hospital where patients with chronic conditions come for up to three months to receive care. These typically aren't your acutely ill patients: these are the ones who are in critical condition. Some are on the brink of death.

This place was never known by the community as a place where you would want to reside. It was known in the community as a "place known for death." It was not very appealing to say the least. But I didn't look around at my surroundings as a place known for death. But I looked within myself because this was where I could plant seeds in a garden. God was going to use me, and use me He did.

The facility was a forty-bed unit. Within the unit were six critical beds for mechanical ventilators and the rest for chronic illnesses, such as diabetes, kidney failure, dialysis patients, chronic wounds, and extreme motor vehicle accidents. We had everything a normal hospital would have had. We had physical therapists, speech therapists, occupational therapists, social workers, respiratory therapists, nurses, physicians, and so forth.

I grew great relationships with my coworkers. Some of them I knew from working at the primary hospital in

Joplin. Some I built new relationships with. Over time, once I planted myself deep within the soil and built trust with others around me, the seed that I was carrying had no choice but to scatter among the people there.

Claire was one of the nurses. I knew Claire from working in the emergency department previously. She was always seemingly quiet, yet at times I found her opening up about her beliefs. Every morning before I went into work I always prayed, "God, use me to minister at work and to reach the people who you place in my path today." I prayed this prayer every morning before I opened the doors to this facility.

Claire was a woman who grew up in the church as a child. She had a beautiful family—a husband and two children. She told me she had not been to church in almost fourteen years. One day, I was randomly doodling a Scripture on a piece of paper at my desk. The call light had gone off as I answered the call light in the patient's room across from me. After I had left the room, I saw something so profound. Claire was sitting there in awe at my desk reading the Scripture I had written.

"How can you love God?" Claire questioned.

I looked back at her puzzled as I had never been asked that question before. *How do you love God?* I pondered. Have you ever been asked that question? Sometimes people will ask questions that you yourself may have never examined before, thoroughly. Nevertheless, I responded in the best way I knew how: I make God my priority. I get into His Word daily and pray for direction and understanding.

I follow His commands. I make an attempt to speak with Him on a regular basis. These were the best answers I had for her.

You should have seen the gears that were turning in her mind that day. She was never presented with these things during the duration of her life until now. She didn't know what it meant to love God and be loved by Him. She couldn't grasp that there was a God who loved her, unconditionally. She couldn't fathom living a life so abandoned, so dedicated, so transformed, and so eager to know God in this way. She was having seeds planted in her life, and she was witnessing truth for the first time.

Later that day after hours of conversation, I went home and saw my Bible resting on the nightstand. The Holy Spirit told me specifically to give it to her, and the next day I found her in the break room sitting by herself.

"Here, I want to give this to you." I announced.

"Wow, thank you. I'm not sure what to do with it," she responded.

"Start in Matthew. That will be the beginning point for you," I suggested.

That's all I had to do that day. Plant a seed. Give her something she never had before and allow God to do the rest. Over time I started noticing changes in her life. She appeared to be a little peppier and more personable, and she was seeking more answers, which I was delighted to give her. She told me that she had started texting her mother again and was sharing the news I was telling her. She was excited to tell mom that I had given her a Bible. Life changing.

You see, all you have to do is start planting seeds. Start giving people what you have. Share the gospel around you. Give people a chance at purpose. It doesn't take much, but it does take you being obedient to the garden around you—planting, watering, sowing, and one day reaping. Maybe you have a family member who doesn't know Jesus. Maybe you have a neighbor going through some difficult things. Maybe you have a coworker who feels hopeless about life. All it takes is the little seed planted deep within you and scattered among others. But I wasn't there for just Claire: there were so many others who needed what I carried.

Sickness was not a term used in this place because so many people were on the brink of death. A woman, who was currently on a mechanical ventilator, had just heard that her own son had passed away. She was overwhelmed as she was in the middle of losing her own life. But nevertheless, I went into her room on the day that I heard the tragic news. This was a woman who was losing her own life, and yet she had just heard that her son had lost his.

She lipped to me through the tube how sad she was that her son had just died. I asked if I could pray for her. She agreed. As I was praying, I felt the Spirit of God fill the room, and in return she had a smile on her face and was overwhelmed with emotion. God was turning her grief into grace! She thanked me so much for the prayers and kindness.

Shortly after, the call light to one of my patient's room went off. I entered the room. This was a young man who was on a mechanical ventilator as well. He had overdosed on alcohol and pills and was on life support because of it. He was alert enough to understand and communicate. He wrote on a piece of paper that he had been suffering from suicidal thoughts all his life. And here he felt himself in the worst predicament.

My response to him was that there was a reason why he was still alive and that he had purpose. He agreed and was listening. I asked if I could pray for him. He eagerly wanted prayer. Then, I looked over beside his bed and found a Bible opened up to Ephesians 3, which I coincidently had been reading that morning! I started reading it and teaching him what it meant. He was so encouraged that throughout the day instead of hitting his call light for care, he was hitting his call light for me to read more of God's Word to him. Amazing!

As you can see, seeds were being scattered in that place, and I witnessed it firsthand. Not only was this encouraging to people around me, but it gave me purpose as well. Sowing seeds is a part of your burn notice. If you want to ignite a flame, start by seed planting around you. What garden are you currently in? Have you found ways to scatter your seed in people? Are you seeing fruit? Everybody around you is looking for encouragement. They ultimately are looking for an encounter with God. The real question is: are you going to supply this demand?

Find ways to scatter seed in the current environment you are in. It may be that some seed reaps a hundred-fold, some sixty-fold, or some thirty-fold, but whatever the reward is, know that you are scattering out of obedience to God, not for personal gain. That's the thing: once you scatter some seed, more seed will be granted to you. And eventually that seed has no choice but to reap a good harvest. Your reward will come when you least expect it.

The Salvage Yard

Serving on the streets quickly became a magnet that drew people in from all walks of life. Every week we provided a meal, a message, and hope. In fact, that became our name, S.O.S. Ministries (Serving on the Streets), Inc. It's revelational how we came up with the name.

My wife and I had journeyed out to a small town for a quick getaway. While there, there was a symbol we kept running into—an anchor. We saw it on T-shirts, window displays, retail shelves, everywhere. I bet I counted seeing this unfamiliar anchor over thirty times during our little adventure. So, we came home and brainstormed. It was too eye-opening not to.

An anchor, what did it represent? We delved into the Word of God and stumbled upon Hebrews 6:19 that says, "This *hope* we have as an anchor of the soul, both sure and steadfast, and which enters the *Presence* behind the veil." That was it! We knew that what we were doing in the streets was providing hope to anyone who would receive it. Even the ones who didn't receive it initially, eventually saw authentic love. We knew that we were hope dealers who had set up shop in the middle of a park without walls. Even more, what were we doing? Serving on the streets. Serving. On. The. Streets. S.O.S. Ministries. Wow! Not only were we providing hope to the hopeless, but we were a distress call—like Morse code. People were signaling for someone to come and save them. And rescue them we did.

We went from serving a meal to speaking the Word of God over them, to praying and seeing miracles, and now people were asking to be baptized. Not a come to the stage for an altar call, they were approaching us and begging us to be baptized! Unheard of. So, we started baptizing people who were coming off the streets. They were various people from different walks of life. Some were homeless. Some were poor. Others were receiving and finding love— something really real. We were a lighthouse on top of a hill, and we had no form of advertisement. It was word of mouth. And it got out quickly.

We were consistently feeding and ministering to 200 people every Sunday. This became overwhelming for us as a group, and we knew that we were on to something big. So, what better way than to get the local churches involved? We prayed and asked the Lord to send the laborers for the harvest that was ripe. And wouldn't you know it, churches started calling us when they heard what we were doing. We were planting good seed in good soil. We were gathering churches and empowering them to love the poor. Though it was a very unstable environment, one they had never resonated in before, they felt the love of Christ and the power of the kingdom here.

Some Sundays there would be just an overwhelming peace. Other Sundays there would be shakable miracles. That's just it. I was actually witnessing what I believed to be the kingdom of God that you read about in the Bible. I was seeing the hand of Jesus sweep through the crowd. I saw Jesus, not only in the people serving but also in the eyes of the homeless. These people had nothing to offer, yet they had something a lot of people didn't—extreme faith. "Blessed *are* the poor in spirit, For theirs is the kingdom of heaven" (Matthew 5:3).

We were advancing to a point where we had many churches involved and donations coming in from people in all walks of life, yet we knew winter was coming.

I don't know if you are familiar with Missouri weather, but during the colder months it can reach negative temperatures. And without any walls, it can be very difficult to serve in the streets. So, we asked God for a place where we could continue to serve the community. It wouldn't take long for us to get a call.

I answered my phone from a local ministry already working here downtown. It was called the Salvage Yard. I know what you're thinking, how can a salvage yard with wrecked cars and unstable grounds be a place where you can serve people? It wasn't your typical defined salvage yard, it was a facility where their mission was to get people out of the bar district and into a contemporary, very inviting place to learn more about God.

They had open mic nights, a coffee bar, pool tables, and flat screens to watch sporting games. It was very urban here and reminded me of a poetry bar where you would orally recite your inspirational messages. The lights were dimmed. The stage looked like what you would see at a rock concert, but it had one eye-appealing logo: there were anchors everywhere! Not just the anchors, but the Scripture quoted directly from Hebrews 6:19, "This hope we have as an anchor of the soul." *Was I dreaming here? Was this really happening?*

I was literally standing in the middle of the building, panning around at the canvases I was seeing. I could not believe I was witnessing the very thing we had been working on, and God was revealing His nature to us. He kind of likes to show off like that. This place was perfect for us. It had seating, tables, fish tanks, and an area to set up the food. And, even more surreal, I knew the director of the facility!

Sam and I go way back. He used to be a drummer deep within the secular world, and I was a prep deep within the partying community. Both of us were on a reckless path, and now we were both on the right path with a connective purpose. I told him about what we were doing. He loved it. In fact, he handed us the keys to the building that night. Say what?!?

The Salvage Yard gave us full permission to serve the people in the community every Sunday afternoon. It quickly became our home. We made the transition over the next couple of weeks, letting the people know we would be moving to a new location. I enjoyed the streets. But these streets would have to wait because frostbite isn't appealing.

We didn't know how well the people would adapt to the new building. I mean, you have to understand that these people were the ones who would never step foot into a church. That's a good word for what we were doing:

churching the unchurched. The good news is this building was located on the Main Street of downtown Joplin near the homeless shelters. But again, we weren't just serving the homeless. Soon, people from all sorts of backgrounds would be entering these walls.

Anytime we transitioned, there would always be a drop in the numbers. Mainly because word had not gotten out completely. But when you become a lighthouse, eventually people will be drawn to your light. Quickly people started hearing about the Salvage Yard. We had beautiful music playing over the speakers, a stage to present the Word of God, and tables to serve the people. Once our doors opened, we greeted every individual with a smile and a welcoming heart. I would shake the hands of the crippled, the unbathed, those with scraggly beards, the backpackers, women and children. We had one primary focus: to be an epicenter of love.

These people were pushed out by the public, overlooked by the city, and lowered to a below-the-standard type status. These people yearned for acceptance. They yearned to be recognized. And we yearned to dish out love to everyone we came into contact with. The Salvage Yard was becoming a host of lost souls, where we came together to salvage dead things, salvage brokenness, and revive lives.

If you wanted to put a title on what the Salvage Yard was, it was an emergency department for the lost. People came in initially to receive a meal, but when they entered these premises, they felt something different. Most responded with, "There is something here. Something I am feeling. I can't quite put my finger on it, but I know it's good." To be verbally honest, they were feeling the love of the Father for the first time. And that is exactly what we were wanting to give them—the love of the Father.

Jesus says in John 13:34, "A new commandment I give to you, that you love one another; as I have loved you, that you also love one another." That was it. It wasn't designing some fancy logo to lure people into our church. It wasn't spending more money on lighting and sound to give people the experience of a concert. It was loving them to the very core. We used food as bait, but God used His Spirit for the catch! After all, "Then He [Jesus] said to them, "Follow Me, and I will make you fishers of men" (Matthew 4:19).

The Salvage Yard over the next few months grew and grew. There were times where we didn't have seating, nor did we probably comply with fire codes, but somehow, some way, there was always room. Churches started calling and asking to be a part of this movement. And even though we really had no idea how much food to prepare, somehow, we always had enough food. Supernaturally, sometimes we literally would serve the last plate to an individual who straggled in the door late. This would only fuel our faith.

The Salvage Yard became so brightly equipped that it radiated out into the streets. We heard of people who were living in garages and coming in. Others were neighbors who were living within walking distance. Parents showed up in vans full of children who had been living in their vehicles. Everyone. For me, I was continually seeing what Jesus kept talking about to His disciples, "Let your light so shine before men, that they may see your good works and glorify your Father in heaven" (Matthew 5:16).

One day we had an extremely large turnout. The people filled all the way to the walls as if the building would explode at any moment. I'm not a numbers kind of guy, but I would assume there were well over 200 people there and even more outside. After I finished preaching the Word of God to the congregation, a staff member grabbed me. He told me there was a man outside who he needed me to speak with him. I walked through the crowd to find a man on a bench. He was in a position focused downward at the ground. Once I was within an arm's reach, he looked up at me with the most heart-filled words, "I have *got* to find this Jesus."

With an amazed look on my face I asked the question, "Do you know Christ?" He told me he did at one point in his life but that he had lost Him along the way. The Spirit of God overtook me, and I told him about the love of God and the relationship we are invited into with Him. I literally was giving him the gospel. And then, right in the middle of all the people, he rededicated his life to God as the crowd around us applauded. He had tears running down his face.

Shortly after he gave his life to Christ, he and his girlfriend kept coming to the Salvage Yard, inspired by what was happening here in the community. They went from being served to serving others. That is the ultimate way! Jonathan was his name, and in a short while he landed a job. He was able to provide for his family and was living a life for the Lord.

So many stories unfolded at the Salvage Yard. Mothers were reconciled with their children. Men laid down their addictions and became fathers once again. Marriages were reconciled. Power and miracles effortlessly manifested themselves throughout the people, and our faith was being taken to new levels. The Salvage Yard wasn't just a Sunday feeding, but it was a glimpse at the kingdom of God. Heaven being exemplified here on earth. We had planted good seeds, and now we were seeing that seed come to life.

Even believers from different countries had tasted that God was good. A man in the crowd, who I knew didn't seem like a frequent attendee, was sitting in the background. After the service, he approached me and said, "Hi, I'm Jacque." Jacque was a casually dressed man with a good haircut. He wore fine jewelry and even a good pair of glasses. He went on to tell me about an interesting story on how he had gotten here.

Jacque was a truck driver all the way from Canada. He exported goods and supplies from Canada and transported them to the United States. It was Jacque's day off today. Instead of sitting in his truck watching movies, he wanted to do something for God. So, he prayed and asked the Lord what He wanted him to do.

Then Jacque felt a sudden urge to go for a walk.

While walking down a main road, it started to downpour. Great. He was too far from his vehicle to turn back. Then, suddenly, a vehicle pulled over and asked if he could give him a ride. Jacque, not knowing what he should do, involuntarily hopped into the vehicle. The driver asked where he was going.

"Not sure," Jacque replied.

The driver asked if Jacque wanted to go to a feeding. Jacque agreed. Jacque shared that story with me of how he had ended up here at the Salvage Yard that day. We were able to sit and fellowship and talk about all the good things God had done in our lives. We got to pray for his marriage, and he prayed for the ministry. From Canada all the way to the Salvage Yard, Jacque wanted to know what God had for him today. And knowingly, it was to fellowship with other believers as well as to understand the significance of God's direction when we faithfully begin to ask Him questions, such as, "Where do you want me to go today, God?" Try asking yourself that same question now.

This was our garden. We were planting seeds in many people who spread throughout the community. You never know really where that seed will go. But as Paul says, "I planted, Apollos watered, but God gave the increase. So then neither he who plants is anything, nor he who waters, but God who gives the increase" (1 Corinthians 3:5–7).

And then, suddenly, the Salvage Yard would be closing their doors.

It was shocking, to say the least, when Sam sat me down to tell me the Salvage Yard would be closing their doors. They just didn't have the finances to keep it open. I understood, but with so much sustenance happening here, I was disappointed to say the least. Nevertheless, I honored the Salvage Yard's leadership for allowing us to use their facility. We had told them that we would just stay for the winter, but that time had increased and become a full year.

During one of the last weeks at the Salvage Yard, we broke the news to the community. Many were sad. But with boldness we came together, praying that God would give us a new location. I knew we wouldn't go back to the streets just yet. But how could we afford something? We barely had any money, and the Salvage Yard had allowed us to use their facility for free. I knew there wouldn't be another organization that would allow us to use their facility rent free, but that didn't matter. We kept praying anyway.

The final two weeks had approached for the Salvage Yard to close down. We were scrambling like a bunch of newborn chicks, attempting to find our warm home. Prayer was like a lifeline for us. We would pray individually. We would pray as a ministry. And we would pray as a congregation. We just didn't have any answers from God.

Later that week, my wife had checked the mail one day at our house. In it was a letter from an unknown address. The letter was from a local woman who had heard about our ministry. She stated in her letter that her family had received an inheritance check. Unsure of where this letter was going, she continued to tell us that our ministry was weighing deep within her heart and that God told her to give us a portion of the inheritance. Enclosed with the letter was a $5,000 check! I lost it. I fell to my knees, and my wife and I couldn't hold back the tears. We were so grateful. I don't even think I could really put it into emotions, all I knew was God was so reliable. He was reassuring us that we were on the right path and that the seeds we planted were reaping a harvest. How great is our God?

Oh yeah, after we gathered ourselves from the mountain of tissues, we looked again at the top of the check. Right along the left corner of the check was the lady's address. Can you guess what her address was? The road she lived on—are you ready for this—was "Simplicity Way." Unbelievable!

Marching Orders

I hope you have gathered a lot of good seed that was planted here in this chapter. Two things: make sure the first seed you plant is God's seed in your own life, and second, start planting seed within people. It doesn't have to sprout initially. All you have to do is be obedient to delivering the seed. Some plant, others till, many water, and some reap. But God gives the increase! Being a seed sower is a vital part of your faith. We are either holding on to seed or we are scattering good seed. It is ultimately our choice. Through our experiences with God and in knowing that He is a good, good Father, we should be spreading this gift to others. A seed, an encouraging word, an act of obedience, and reshaping people's lives all work toward increasing the kingdom of God. There really is no better way than to manage your own garden God has given you and see this garden spread throughout your life! Go scatter and then gather.

CHAPTER 5

Transformation > Change

P. T. Barnum was an American promotor, born on July 5, 1810, in the city of Bethel, Connecticut. As a young boy, he fell into the depths of poverty. A natural salesman, he peddled snacks and cherry rum to soldiers by age twelve as a form of income. If there was one thing that P. T. Barnum exemplified as a young man, it was *drive*. He believed that deep down inside himself was a spectacular nuance. Rightfully so, he continued in his search for success.

Over time, he developed into a young man and moved to New York City and tried his hand at a variety of businesses, including newspaper publishing and running a boarding house. Though his temporary careers seemed to collect a variety of incomes, he was moved by the extraordinary.

In 1841 he purchased an old, beat-up American Museum to persuade people to witness the beauty of different spectacles. Unfortunately, people didn't bite at his unforeseen imagination. He wanted people to be awed, to be overwhelmed, and to see beauty in the history of collective art. But still, tickets didn't sell, and the doors were soon to be closed.

Suddenly, he saw people who were living in the cracks of life being pushed out by the public because of their anomalies. Most spectators saw them and categorized them as "misfits of nature." They were different than your normal, so-called human beings. They had characteristics about themselves that illustrated *outsiders*. But still, P. T. Barnum saw something miraculous in them that could be siphoned out for a higher calling.

Annie Jones, known as the Bearded Lady, caught P. T. Barnum's eye by her overgrown facial hair. He looked past the grungy mass of balled hair growing from underneath her chin. No one in this generation had seen a woman with facial hair. Women were seen as petite, well groomed, and softly spoken. But not Annie Jones, she was too manly for the public.

Or there was Charles Stratton, famous as General Tom Thumb, measuring in at no more than three foot tall. He was not acceptably inclined by his height, to say the least. People literally looked over him his entire life, and this only brought feelings of being an outcast from his peers around him. Jobless and rebuked by the public, he found himself partnering up with P. T. Barnum. And he was lifted to a higher calling.

There's even Chang & Eng. born in Thailand, who were conjoined twins since birth. Called the Siamese Twins because of their home place, they, too, were neglected because of their anomaly nature and unforeseen physical appearance. But not with P. T. Barnum because he saw beauty in the beasts.

Collectively, P. T. Barnum began searching for these "human curiosities" because what he envisioned was an assembly of unnatural humans who could be put into show business and display their daunting physical appearance. He saw success in the unsuccessful. He saw imagination in the unimaginable. What he wanted was to take what was naturally given to them and ignite impossible success.

He didn't want to change one thing about who they were, but he wanted to transform who they had already become! And overnight this anomaly-type show became a success. Though ticket holders were drawn to see these human curiosities, it was giving the people purpose! Those who were once lost were now being found. Those who were once outcasts were now being accepted, using their characteristics as a tool to exemplify their God-given abnormalities.

P. T. Barnum's burn notice was to transform people's lives as a showcase, allowing them to use their talents to bring what was dead (emotionally) to life! The show kept growing. The ticket sales usually sold out. P. T. Barnum was soon becoming "The Greatest Showman" of their time, and he was burning with passion to give people purpose regardless of their disabilities. Handicaps were nonexistent in his eyes. What he was seeing was beauty, and they soon were becoming family. Closely-knit together by love and wonder, they were transformed among the crowds.

P. T. Barnum went on to serve two terms as legislature for Connecticut in 1865. He was part of the ratification of the Thirteenth Amendment to abolish slavery. He was elected to improve the water supply, bring gas lighting to the streets, enforce liquor and prostitution laws, and was instrumental in starting Bridgeport Hospital, which was founded in 1878.

Needless to say, P. T. Barnum became an icon for the people. He helped others to find their purpose while creating opportunity for his own path. His passion resonated in the hearts of the human curiosities, and he brought change to the nation. P. T. Barnum himself was transformed in the process. As he spoke to the legislature, in front of many politicians, he said these words, "A human soul, that God has created and Christ died for, is not to be trifled with."[1]

P. T. Barnum's understanding of creation is that God made it and we are to attain it. "How beautiful upon the mountains Are the feet of him who bring good news, Who proclaim peace, Who bring good news, Who proclaims peace, Who brings glad tidings of good *things*, Who proclaims salvation, Who says to Zion, 'Your God reigns!'" (Isaiah 52:7).

We are to be transformers who find people in the cracks—people who are searching for a calling and need hope. Change is inevitable. We understand that seasons change, jobs change, and people change, but those who bring transformation find new life. Not only do we transform others around us, but we are being transformed in the process.

This is where we begin to understand that change is less than transformation. Transformation always trumps change because change only brings about returned patterns and cycles. Have you ever felt like you were stuck in a pattern? A cycle of hopelessness? Searching for a way out? The Bible goes on to say, "And do not be conformed to this world, but be transformed by the renewing of your mind, that you may prove what *is* that good and acceptable and perfect will of God" (Romans 12:2). This is the first step toward transformation, when we use our minds to take us to new heights. Let's explore.

Transformation of the Mind

Let's resonate with Romans 12:2, "And do not be conformed to this world, but be transformed by the renewing of your mind. . . ." Siphoning out the word transformed, we find it in the Greek meaning *metamorphoo*. It is pronounced *met-am-or-fo-o* and means to transfigure or to change into another form.[2] In the context of Romans 12:2, it is the obligation of undergoing a complete change, which under the power of God will find expression in character and conduct. *Morphe* lays stress on the inward change.

So, you see, the first step toward transformation begins with the *inward* change. It is the inward man that God is concerned about. "But the LORD said to Samuel, "Do not look at his appearance or his physical stature, because I have refused him. For *the LORD does* not *see* as man sees; for man looks at the outward appearance, but the Lord looks at the heart" (1 Samuel 16:7). It doesn't matter what the outside of your life looks like: if you are not being transformed internally, then there will be no significant change but only superficial redundancy.

According to Scripture, we must be transformed by the *renewing* of our minds. What does that look like? The Greek meaning for renewing is *anakainosis*. It is pronounced *an-ak-ah'-ee-no-ss*. This is the adjustment of the moral and spiritual vision and thinking to the mind of God, which is designed to have a transforming effect upon the life.[3] Did you catch that? Thinking to the *mind* of God! This is the willing response on the part of the believer. Paul writes in Colossians 3:2, "Set your minds on things above, not on things on the earth."

There is a prime example of this Scripture and what Jesus was portraying to others. Nicodemus was a high priest, Pharisee, and ruler of the Jews. Although he was considered a godly man by others, there was an inward cry to find truth in the Son of Man. Never did he dare to ask Jesus for advice because the other Pharisees would have scourged him for doing so. "This man came to Jesus by night and said to Him, 'Rabbi, we know that You are a teacher come from God; for no one can do these signs that You do unless God is with him.' Jesus answered and said to him, 'Most assuredly, I say to you, unless one is born again, he cannot see the kingdom of God'" (John 3:3).

I can see Nicodemus's wheels spinning in his head because it went against everything he read in the Old Testament and everything the legalists spoke about. And I love Nicodemus's scrambled thoughts: "Nicodemus said to Him, 'How can a man be born when he is old? Can he enter a second time into his mother's womb and be born?'" (John 3:3–4). *Like Jesus, how can I be birthed twice? This is just crazy talk. I'm going to have to take an Excedrin Migraine because my head is pounding.*

Nicodemus was missing the whole point. Jesus wasn't talking about physical rebirth, He was Fatherly teaching His children about spiritual rebirth! "Jesus answered and said to him, 'Most assuredly, I say to you, unless one is born of water and Spirit, he cannot enter the kingdom of God. That which is born of the flesh is flesh, and that which is born of the Spirit is spirit. Do not marvel that I have said to you, "You must be born again." The wind blows where it wishes, and you hear the sound of it, but cannot tell where it comes from and where it goes. So is everyone who is born of the Spirit'" (John 3:5–8).

What God wants us to understand is that there are two births to our lives. The first birth is done by water, when we are physically birthed out of our mother's womb. The second, and this is the most profound, is the spiritual rebirth! In order for our lives to transform, we must be reborn again. When we say "yes" to Jesus and "no" to this world, we are either conforming to something that never belonged to us in the first place or we are being transformed into the image of Christ—who we were meant to live like.

Nicodemus still puzzled, so "Jesus answered and said to him, 'Are you the teacher of Israel, and do not know these things?' Most assuredly, I say to you, We speak what We know and testify what We have seen, and you do not receive Our witness. If I told you earthly things and you do not believe, how will you believe if I tell you heavenly things?" (John 3:10–12).

There it is. If you can't believe earthly things, how will you believe heavenly things? Nicodemus was not transformed. He was only conformed to his religious way of thinking. He was thinking on a worldly perspective. This is where the umbrella of transformation cannot take place. It is the disbelief by our human way of thinking that prevents us from our heavenly calling. Nicodemus believed in God and was a leader for God, but he lacked the one thing Jesus commanded, being born again!

Listen to Paul again in Colossians 3:2–3, "Set your minds on things above, not on things on the earth. For you died, and your life is hidden with Christ in God." Stop using your inhibited mind that produces no transformation. Start thinking like the mind of God, which surpasses all understanding, who gives wisdom to the unintelligent. You must be reborn again to live this life, not through the lens of our old ways but rebirthed by thinking on things above.

The first characteristic toward a transformed life is a transformed mind. Wake up every day knowing that you are loved and that God has a perfect plan for your life. Don't miss this part. It's your mind that obstructs His calling for your life. "For God has not given us a spirit of fear, but of power and of love and of a sound mind" (2 Timothy 1:7). It's fear that pushes us back. But God is calling forth individuals who will announce their rebirth.

That's the thing, perfect love pushes out fear. "There is no fear in love' but perfect love casts out fear, because fear involves torment. But he who fears has not been made perfect in love" (1 John 4:18). What is it that your dealing with right now? Is it fear? Uncertainty? Dissatisfaction? Loss of hope? When you have a transformed mind, you are no longer compromising with your feelings, but you are functioning with your faith. Faith comes from God, and God is eternal. So, when you believe that God can do all things in your life, you have the mindset of a heavenly realm and have stepped foot into a new dimension. You are thinking like Him.

"But without faith *it is* impossible to please *Him*, for he who comes to God must believe that He is, and *that* He is a rewarder of those who diligently seek Him" (Hebrews 11:6). We must not fear because fear is a feeling of this world. It's the weightiness of your finances, the blockade of performing for others, and the lies and voices that tell you you're not good enough, strong enough, smart enough, or talented enough to conquer this world. Listen to Jesus: "My sheep hear My voice, and I know them, and they follow Me. And I give them eternal life, and they shall never perish;

neither shall anyone snatch them out of My hand" (John 10:27–28).

Fear is a virus that invades our minds. It is destructive, and it is discomforting. But Jesus says, "Be reborn again!" Re-dream again. Re-adventure again. Be reborn and see the catalyst erupt from the inside out. This is where transformation gravitates when we push fear and feelings aside and put on the armor of God. God tells us that our faith is more genuine than gold.

Nicodemus digested the words of Jesus and carried them back to his temple. What happened next we do not fully know. But the truth is that he had an encounter with the Man who was the prime example of rebirth. He was the spokesman for it. Jesus was the billboard for God, and His prime teaching was centered around being born again.

If we are to transform, we must adjust our spiritual vision and thinking to the mind of God, who gives good gifts to His children. His promises are never ending, and His ways of thinking are eternal and never fade away. What if you awakened today thinking like God? What if you pushed aside your old way of thinking? What if you believed you could do all things? Speak healing into existence? Transform lives around you? Do all things? Obtain all things? Experience all things? This is where we go from thinking to living.

Transformation of the Body

I'm going to be frank with you: I love to work out. I'm like a workout-oholic. I have spent a majority of my life in the gym. My father inspired me by buying a rugged, cheap bench press that he placed in the center of our garage. I was always scrawny in stature, so my father took the initiative to bulk me up.

I started with the bar and worked my way up plate-upon-plate. Over time my muscles started to develop, and my confidence was boosted in the process. It became a passion of mine. I thought, *How cool is it that I can lift weight and see my body be transformed in the process.*

As I was entering high school, I joined the wrestling team. I'm not 100 percent certain why, but I wanted to use my muscles to gain medals. I was 103 pounds my freshmen year. I didn't stutter here, I was a lean, undersized figurine of a fighter. What they didn't tell me about wrestling is that guys cut weight. This went against every belief I had as I was wanting to gain size not lose size. But, nevertheless, the sport became a passion of mine.

After high school and learning what it was like to be an adult, I got back into the weight room and increased in size once again. It took me awhile to gain my size back in high school. It was my senior year before I put back on about forty pounds. And it wasn't until in adulthood that I gained a few more. Fast forwarding, I lifted weights for approximately fifteen years of my life. That's a lot of gym time! But what happened over the course of those years was that I wasn't gaining any more mass or muscle. I was stagnant. I was seeing no more progression. In fact, I seemed to be losing strength instead of gaining strength.

Then one day a buddy of mine asked me to come to a local CrossFit gym. If you are thinking what I was thinking,

Oh, here we go, another CrossFit junky. You know how you can tell whether someone does CrossFit? They talk about it (joke inserted here). So, I agreed to go for a free workout that morning at 5:00 a.m. Ugh!

If I had to describe the workout in one word, it would be *gross.* That's a good word for it. I remembered, at one point, that my vision came closing in. I was losing oxygen! I went home that day aching and uncomfortable for the first hour. But after the duration of that hour, I had an insurmountable amount of energy! Say what?!?

By my bad decision I went back to that gym over and over, feeling the pain and anguish of CrossFit. It's like it was destroying me from the inside out. But I kept feeling great afterwards! Sure, there was pain, but eventually there was significance. In due time, I became a member of CrossFit and have been doing it ever since. It has changed my life physically.

I didn't see body transformation at first, but in due time I saw gains. I was beginning to see more muscle tone. My strength was going up. The movements I couldn't do before I now could do. Man, was my physical body being transformed! It took long and hard work, but I eventually saw a significant amount of great results. I was accomplishing more than I had ever scratched the surface of accomplishing in a weight gym.

There was a manifestation that Peter, James, and John witnessed on a mountaintop. Jesus had led them up the mountain after prophesying of His crucifixion and teaching His disciples to deny themselves, pick up their crosses, and follow Him. That was not a very inviting message to say the least. The disciples were standing there on the mountaintop, "And He was transfigured before them. His face shone like the sun, and His clothes became as white as the light" (Matthew 17:2).

Jesus's body was literally transformed before the eyes of His followers, and they couldn't bear it. "While he was still speaking, behold, a bright cloud overshadowing them; and suddenly the voice came out of the cloud, saying, 'This is My beloved Son, in whom I am well pleased. Hear Him!'" (Matthew 17:5). The disciples fell on their faces and were greatly afraid. "But Jesus came and touched them and said, 'Arise, and do not be afraid'" (Matthew 17:7).

This was the first time Jesus's body was transformed before the eyes of His followers. It is a prime example of how we should be transformed in our bodies. First, there is the transformation of our minds and then the transformation of our bodies. The Bible also says, "You are light of the world. A city that is set on a hill cannot be hidden. Nor do they light a lamp and put it under a basket, but on a lampstand, and it gives light to all who are in the house" (Matthew 5:14–15). And that God is the, ". . . Father of lights, with whom there is no variation or shadow of turning" (James 1:17).

After your mind is being transformed into the image of God, next comes the transformation of the body. The light that is so illuminated inside you is to be shone for the world to see. Your light is transformation. It has the ability to push out the darkness all around you. And the best part about the light is that people will be attracted to it.

There is the second part about Romans 12:2 that you must understand. The Greek word is *suschematizo*, pronounced *soos-khay-mat-id-zo,* which is the verb behind "to fashion or shape one thing like another."[4] If we are to conform to anything, it is to conform to the pattern of Christ. In due time, we become the image of Christ. This is the byproduct of internal change that exhibits outward transformation. It lays stress on the outward; the present continuous tenses indicate a *process.*[5] Did you catch that? Transformation outwardly is a process. It doesn't happen overnight. It is a continuous push toward being godly, pure, and holy.

It is the transformation by renewing the mind, thinking like God, changing inwardly, and through the process being transformed into the image of Christ! This is true transformation! And it is the way to life.

Take for instance the illustration of my workout life above. Transformation did not happen overnight. In fact, it didn't happen in a couple months. It happened when I least expected it. I was working on my body passionately and eventually the results followed.

When we choose to change our lives and live them for the gospel, transformation takes place. But it doesn't happen overnight. Many people get stuck on the idea of instant transformation. Some are in the initial phase of being a believer. Some have been a believer for decades, and yet, maybe they have not understood the significance of transformation. Some of you are going through seasons of rest, and others are experiencing seasons of harvest. But when we collect one of the most powerful tools in the kingdom of God, and that is transforming into the image of Christ, extraordinary things start to happen.

Let us be transformers of the mind and transformers of the body. "Clearly you are an epistle of Christ, ministered by us, written not with ink but by the Spirit of the living God" (2 Corinthians 3:3). Moses, who had to put a veil over his face because the children of Israel could not look steadily at the light, was physically transformed. We have the ability to shine just as Moses did. Listen to these concluding words, "Nevertheless when one turns to the Lord, the veil is taken away. Now the Lord is Spirit; and where the Spirit of the Lord *is*, there *is* liberty. But we all, with unveiled face, beholding as in a mirror the glory of the Lord, are being transformed into the same image from glory to glory, just as by the Spirit of the Lord" (2 Corinthians 3:16–18). Once the mind and the body are transformed, be ready, there will be a rapid transformation in and around your environment.

Transformation of Life

We have delved into the nature of what it means to transform mind and body. If we are to burn with passion and change the world around us, we must begin to think how God thinks. And if we are to think like God thinks, eventually our expressive nature replicates the inside of our hearts. That is where our outside appearances begin to transform.

From mind to body comes the next best part: the transformation of life and not just the life you live but the lives of others around you. Think of transformation as a contagious virus. Once the fruit of Jesus gets inside you, people will want to come along your tree and pick the fruit from your branches. It's contagious. It replicates. And people begin to transform before your very eyes, only increasing your faith. Let me show you.

I had been working back in the emergency department taking care of acutely ill and critically conditioned patients. I loved the ER—especially because I believed it to be a buffet for the believer. People came in broken. They came in messed up. Some were suicidal. Some were in danger of their lives. What better place to reveal the Spirit of God than in this environment?

A young gentleman came in one afternoon to be seen. He was not your regular, casual patient. This man came in jail attire. He was dressed in all orange, shackles covering both his wrists and ankles, with his head held low. I saw nothing but sadness and brokenness in this man. He was being seen for a medical evaluation.

He claimed that he was trying to commit suicide and didn't want to live anymore because his life had been consumed by tragedy. He had gone through many mishaps in his life and reflected on a lot of why he was in the position he was in now.

While everyone gossiped around me about this man being a loser, I saw him as a son. How unfortunate are we that we can judge people around us and yet not look at our own lives by the mistakes we have made?

I was consumed with God up to this point in my life. I was learning what it meant to be transformed and to transform others around me. I approached the man and drew his blood. The prison guard had followed me as we headed to the x-ray room, shot the image, and clanked our way back to his room.

The prison guard had stepped out of the x-ray room, and I knew this was my chance to speak life to the man.

"I see you, man." I whispered.

"What?" The man replied.

"I see you for who you are. God's son." I proclaimed.

The man then broke down into tears. "I have messed up all my life," the man said, "Done nothing but ruined people's lives and have become a burden to everyone I see."

With my heart heavy and the prison guard outside the door, I knew this was my chance. "Let me pray for you." I continued.

"Yes, please do. I need God more now than ever. I have actually been praying lately for God to save me," he said.

As I began to pray for him, the Spirit of God filled the room. His tears grew larger as if the chains of his life were lifting off his shoulders. He was being changed right before my very eyes.

After we got done praying, the physician entered the room and said, "Sir, your blood work came back normal. Medically, you are free to go."

The prisoner then told me that he really didn't want to kill himself because he was too scared to end his life. Somehow the prison guard, due to the circumstances, had to release him judicially because we were going to have to put him on a suicide hold. The man was okay with this.

We changed him into scrubs, and he was released from his shackles. We sat and talked for some time. I got to hear about his life and the direction it had been going. I told him about my past and that I was now a new creation (transformed). He was inspired and knew his life could be transformed as well.

Just before the hospital security guards took the patient away, I gave him one of my cards.

"Call me when you get better," I encouraged him.

"I definitely will. Thank you so much for caring and giving me a reason to live now," the man replied. And the man left the hospital—unchained, unmonitored by prison guards, and with a grin on his face that showed me hope. I waved as the man left in the distance and disappeared.

Months had gone by, and I was continuing to pray for patients and seeing miraculous signs and wonders. But I couldn't help but think of this man every once in a while. How he was doing? Where was he currently? Had he transformed his life?

Then one day, I got the phone call from an unknown number. "Aaron, it's me—Sam! I wanted to let you know things have changed, and I'm doing so good!"

That was his name, Sam. And his life had been transformed! Shortly after he left the psychological facility and was released, all charges were dropped. He checked into a halfway house for addiction recovery. Not only had he been clean for months, but he had given his life to God and was now a manager over the halfway house, helping other men who were stuck in their addictions.

He was a gifted artist and started painting again. In fact, he started a movement called "The Lord's Paintbrush" where he paints murals on building walls, giving people inspiration and hope and using his talent as a tool for the kingdom. Talk about transformation!

How did he get to this place of change? Well, it took an unforeseen event in the hospital where people who are transformed are contagiously spreading hope and encouragement to others around them. This, ultimately, influences people to become transformed as well, and you can see the finished product—how one act of reaching out created change in another person's heart. Sam's life was miraculously transformed, and now he was a contagion for others.

If you want to transform others, you must be transformed as well. There is no need to attempt transformation. It's seeking your new identity every day. It's getting on your knees and saying, "God, help to transform my life so that I may spread hope to all I come into contact with." It's a process. But over time God will give you more opportunity to spread love everywhere you go.

There was no agenda here. No walls. No judgment. Just love. And as the Scripture proclaims, "Let your light so shine before men, that they may see your good works and glorify your Father in heaven" (Matthew 5:16). You have the ability to shift atmospheres and change culture. The emergency department was my transformation chamber. What's yours? What area does God have you in now where you can be a light? It doesn't have to be a church building. The kingdom of God is within you.

If you are going to burn like never before, you are going to have to step out in faith and fuel others around you. Give them the very thing that is exploding inside you—Jesus. "For it is the power of God who works in you, both to will and to work for *His* good pleasure" (Philippians 2:13).

Sam's life was changed that day, and eventually change brought forth transformation. Sam was given a new identity and a new way to live life to the fullest through a relationship with God. God showed him his passion and his calling, and Sam went forth and multiplied! Astonishing.

Or take my father for instance. He was never the "religious" type. He grew up in a Catholic church with his mother, but through the years he did not attend a church regularly as an adult. My mother and he went to a Methodist church where my mother was highly involved.

My father was not the type who saw significance in going to church every day or maybe in reading his Bible on a regular basis. But he did believe in helping his neighbor. Over the years he did cool things like designing stained glass windows for the church, he was an advocate for Big Brothers Big Sisters, and he used his deer meat to feed the less fortunate. He promoted an outreach life.

Once he got word that we were feeding people in the streets, he wanted to come and check out what all the talk was about. He came and was immediately hooked. He loved the algorithm of preaching the Word of God off a picnic table, feeding the people, and praying for the less fortunate.

One day my father approached me and said, "God is here." It was the first time I saw inspiration in my father's heart. He was moved with compassion, and compassion provokes people to do more. That's the thing: people started showing up to volunteer from all walks of life. Some brought clothes. Others brought money, hand baskets full of hygiene products, and everything in between.

My father was a carpenter by trade. Not that it was his primary career, as he was retired by then, but he was more of a "handyman" who was in desperate need of helping others. One of the observations he made was that these people were always commuting yet had no transportation. He had his "aha" moment and knew he had stored away several bikes that were no longer in use. So, he restored what was broken and began making them like new.

He brought his first finished bike to the feed that next Sunday. He wanted to find out who was truly in need. Low and behold, it didn't take long to find his first client. Once the bike was given to an individual in need, others wanted what he had to offer. People started requesting bikes to help them get to their jobs, to see their families, and to explore the city.

Out of the blue, people started handing him parts. It was as if the flood gates of Niagara Falls lowered the dams and an abundance of supply met the demand. Week after week more bikes were handed out and week after week more testimonies started to follow. I recall one that my father was proud to share.

There was a young woman who was commuting two and a half miles every day to a local fast-food restaurant from the homeless shelter. She didn't care because she was ambitious about working to get off the streets. One day my father overheard about this dedicated woman walking to work and was moved to help her with transportation.

While the woman was working the drive-thru, my father stood outside with the bike while another man told the woman to look outside. As she looked out to the parking lot, she saw the bike with my father waving in the background.

"Is that for me?" The woman questioned.

"Of course!" the man smiled.

She was overwhelmed. She couldn't believe someone had taken the time out of his life to give her this refurbished gift. Best of all, it was all hers now! She was brought to tears. All her hard work was paying off, and now she had an easier way to continue in the pursuit of earning enough money to get her own place. My father was moved. She was wrecked.

This is a prime example of what it means when you begin to transform the lives around you. My father, who really didn't attend church and didn't read much of his Bible, came to an event where he felt the presence of God and was moved to help others. This inevitably transcended forward and touched other lives around him.

Imagine, if you will, a net. You are in a boat, surrounded by a large amount of water. All you have to do is throw the net. You have no clue how much you will catch or the amount. All you have to do is throw it, and the net will eventually catch all kinds of fish. But you won't be catching fish, instead you will be catching men and women.

Jesus said it in Matthew 4:19, ". . . Follow Me, and I will make you fishers of men." Understand that transformation is two things: it is changing your mind to think how God thinks and knowing that this is a process. Once you have conquered these two commands, be ready because lives will transform all around you.

The disciples knew what process meant. The first invitation Jesus gave was to follow Him. At first, the disciples had no clue what they were getting in to. In the three and a half years they had spent with the Savior, they had to follow, learn, obey, listen, and eventually be transformed. Jesus knew what it meant to follow Him and knew the main objective: to transform man into the image of Himself.

So, we ask ourselves, "What does transformation look like for my life?" It's a fair question. There are certain characteristics about you that begin to develop over time. You may not notice it at first, but eventually you will see a pattern. You will see that the old life you lived is now becoming new. Let me suggest a few characteristics that might speak to you.

Transformation Qualities

Things that used to be appealing to you are no longer attractive.

Your behavior starts to change (less negativity, less gossip, less complaining, etc.).

Sin becomes less tasteful.

You begin to put away bad habits.

You are no longer at war within yourself (condemnation, regret, and guilt).

You are less at war with other people (confrontation, backbiting, etc.).

Kindness is expressed everywhere you go.

Faith trumps fear.

Prayer becomes a first language.

There are many other instances that represent transformation. I wanted to share examples of what I have experienced. I have noticed these types of traits routinely in my life, and I believe that if you are experiencing some of these right now, you have peeked into the window of transformation already.

P. T. Barnum was a man on a mission. He was tired of seeing people held to a lower standard than what the world perceived. So, through passion and ambition, he began to find people sitting in the cracks, and he gave them an open hand, saying, "I want to take you on a journey. Come with me and I will show you a whole new world." This is what gave human curiosities a chance to transform their lives. And transform they did!

You have the ability to do the same. Not just changing, because we understand change will happen but potentially will only cycle behaviors and habits that go nowhere, but transforming is the only other option. It's becoming new every day, finding more of yourself behind the curtain, and giving your life as a ransom for the one true God who designed and destined you for greatness.

If we are ever going to find our burn notice, we must transform, not change. Be a lighthouse for others around us who are dim. Dimness is nothing more than faded darkness. Transformed people are those who look for darkness because they identify the overpowering light that consumes the darkness. "For it is the God who commanded light to shine out of darkness, who has shone in our hearts to *give* us the light of the knowledge of the glory of God in the face of Jesus Christ" (2 Corinthians 4:6). That is the perfect definition of transformation. That the face of Christ would mask our faces like *Phantom of the Opera*, except without the stage and an audience.

The disciples were on an adventure with no confirmed finale. Their first step toward Christ was the biggest movement of their lives: it was their burn notice. But it took listening, watching, failing, finding, and waiting for three and a half years before they actually knew what it meant to transform. It was a process. But one day, in the middle of an upper room after the crucifixion of Christ, they would be handed something their minds couldn't retain, the Holy Helper. And it changed everything about their lives and the beginning of what would be the church.

Marching Orders

We understand that transformation takes two things: becoming the image of Christ and the process to get there. Above were a few qualities of transformation that I have identified in my life. I want you to write down some things you have changed. They can be anything from your behavior to the way you treat others and so on. Jot them down and meditate on them. You are a lot further in this journey than you thought. It's safe to say you are probably more mature today than you were ten years ago, one year ago, or even one month ago. It's a process, but never forget where you have come from and the distance God has taken you. If you have fallen, get back up. Don't stop now. Brush yourself off, get back on your horse, and ride into the sunset. Transformation waits for you in the distance.

CHAPTER 6:
The Holy Helper

I know what you are thinking: how do I every expect to find my burn notice, and how do I accomplish the task at hand? These are fair questions. More than just fair, it's the right question! I question a lot of things sometimes, like what I'm going to wear, if the diagnosis I made on that patient was correct, what I'm going to eat for dinner, and whether there was a hole in my underwear when I put my pants on this morning. I'm pretty sure my questions have questions. Don't judge me here.

Finding God in the mix of your everyday life can be challenging. Overcome by the awakening of your snooze button three times (you know what I'm talking about), gathering your children, sending them off to school, making it on time to work, kissing your wife goodbye, finding a workout time, preparing dinner, putting the kids to bed, and trying to find some time to sit down and have a moment to yourself. It's very exhausting.

I should know. I have two children who are in diapers and are only seventeen months apart. One is always wanting my attention, and the other is always wanting a bottle. Sometimes I catch myself going into stellar dad mode by using one hand to prop the bottle in my son's mouth while turning the television on with my right great toe to turn on "Wheels on the bus go round-and-round" for my daughter. It's pretty amazing—you should watch it sometime.

But let's be honest: how do we ever find time for God and what we have been created for? You have probably heard it said that we make a priority of things that are important in our lives. And I would have to agree: I do. Although I am extremely swamped (I used that word because it's a term for beyond busy), I always make time for God. He's my priority.

I like to think of making time for God as similar to a YouTube video. Let me explain. When you watch a video on YouTube, unless you purchased YouTube Premium, there are advertising videos inserted at random times throughout your viewing experience. More than that, there is an advertisement video that typically displays at the beginning of every YouTube video. Thank God for the skip ad button! Advertisements are not what we want: we want the video we clicked on for our viewing pleasure. We don't want to hear nor see the ad because it does nothing more than take us away from what we had scheduled.

The video you have playing is your everyday life. It's what you have scheduled, and it's what you want to view. But there are moments throughout the day where we have some free time to insert extracurricular activities. Finding time for God are those inserted moments where He is speaking and wanting to establish a relationship with you. They are ads where He says, "Looking for more purpose?" "Want to be fulfilled?" "Find happiness?"

The question really is, "Are we going to respond to His voice?" The advertisement that shows up at the beginning of every video is similar to us getting up every morning. When you awaken, make time to sit and be with God. It's not a burden, and you most certainly will not hit the skip ad button because when He speaks, you'll know it. It will change the trajectory of your life.

I love YouTube. A lot! But I love spending time with God even more because I have figured out the meaning to this life: to be known and to know Him. It's the best YouTube television you will ever experience. You are the main character, and He is the producer. Both of you are in sync with one another. Actually, He is so much a part of you that He came and made His home in you. He would never ask you to do anything without first sending you a Helper. Except this is no normal assistant, this is your navigational system that directs your vehicle to the appropriate destination.

He's Here

I wouldn't have merit if I talked about the Holy Helper but never had an encounter with the Holy Helper, so I want to adopt a teaching method called *show and tell*. I want to show you then tell you about my experiences.

A group of us young adults ventured off to a program happening at a church called *Apocalypse*. The name itself is not very inviting, but it was an annual event getting a lot of fluff. We had made our way into the coliseum of the church and found our seats. Our group had to be seated in two different sections as there was not enough room for all of us. I had the pleasure of sitting next to my wonderful wife. Not much was happening during the program. Once the event was coming to a close, the pastor grabbed the mic and asked anyone who was not saved or who needed prayer to make their way to the front where the leaders would meet them.

Being that I knew the young adult pastor of this church, he waved me forward and asked me to pray for the individuals who made their way to the front. I couldn't help but get involved. My wife had the opportunity to pray for the women who came forward, scurrying off to the side with a group of women to pray. My buddy and I had found ourselves at the front of the auditorium but not praying for anyone at this time, just standing. And then it happened.

I had been standing there with my eyes fixated on the pastor still speaking. Suddenly, out of nowhere, I felt this gust of wind blow up from behind me. At first, I just thought the air conditioning had kicked on, but then it got stronger.

My jaws slowly started to move and then went into a full-blown chatter. But I wasn't cold. Not at all. Shortly after my body started to shake uncontrollably. I thought, *What was happening to my body? Was I having a seizure? Tremors? Losing my mind?*

Not long after I caught myself in a full-blown body trembling movement, I felt the pure serenity of a different presence. My buddy looked over at me during this time.

"Are you alright, bro?" He asked.

"He's here!" I responded. "God is here!"

I had felt a high like never before. Honestly, I was never so clear minded, closely felt, confidently knowing God was right there with me. He was touching me tangibly for my first time.

My buddy had reached over to grip me close to his body and had started praying. I was like sizzling bacon in his arms, shaking back and forth and unable to control my body. And the tears just started coming, not tears of sadness but tears of joy. For the first time in my life, I was having a tangible experience with God. He was showing Himself to me like never before. And let me tell you, it takes your faith to new heights!

I would go on to say the experience lasted for a good five minutes, but the after effect went on well into the night. I remember shouting to my friends, "How could people not want this?" I was literally on a different wavelength. I like to call it my eternal soundwave. I just kept shouting, "How could people not want this?"

Have you ever had an actual encounter with God? Some of you may have, and some of you may not have. But I would tell you, I didn't get this experience from sitting on a couch watching YouTube, but I got this experience from *seeking* the Lord and going after Him. "Ask, and it will be given to you; seek and you will find; knock and the door will be opened to you" (Matthew 7:7). Have you been seeking? Have you been knocking? Maybe you have been searching for years, but you have never felt the love of God. I will say this: keep seeking and keep knocking. Just when you least expect it, boom! It will happen! I promise you.

Into the Eyes of a Distressed Man

I know I have told you this before, but the emergency department is a place of upmost hopelessness and yet all the opportunity a believer could hope for. I had left my imprint on this unbalanced environment. If you have ever experienced the environment of the emergency room, you will admit that it can change in an instant.

I had just started my shift in the ER, working down in the blue pod. This pod mainly consisted of acutely ill medical patients, dialysis patients, and everything in between. If you have ever heard of a code blue, where a patient's breath and heart stop beating, this was the place where that patient would reside.

We had just received a call from the EMS crew that a middle-aged man was on his way in critical condition for stroke-like symptoms. Moments later we would collide with this man and the ambulance staff. He had been strapped into the stretcher with an oxygen mask applied to his face. His eyes were open, and yet, it appeared as if no one was home.

Just behind him was his wife, and the family was waiting patiently in the waiting room. As a group of ER staff surrounded him like a pack of wolves, we headed down to room thirty-one. Just so we are clear here, rooms thirty and thirty-one are places where the most critically ill are examined and either intubated with a breathing tube or put on drips to keep them alive. This typically was never a good sign.

As multiple physicians surrounded him, they noticed initially that the patient had left-sided facial droop, paralysis, and was unable to speak. Immediately we all turned to one another and knew he was having a stroke. IVs were started, blood was drawn, and he needed a Cat Scan STAT.

So, we disconnected the patient from all the monitors and headed for the CT suite. But something happened along the way. All the staff began to disappear into the background, and I found myself alone with the man. This was not normal protocol as there would always need to be at least three staff transporting together.

Instead of the doctors ordering a STAT CT, they wanted an MRI instead because the patient was almost outside the window of a stroke protocol. This protocol states that anyone who was outside the window of four hours or more from their initial symptoms, would be too late for medication intervention.

God knows the window to the point of no return. And yet, God also knows the power of impossibility. He rests there. Outside our every move and our every doubt, God loves to show His power during our own uncertainty.

As I turned the corner, I knew this was a divine encounter with the Holy Helper. He was with me, and it was my duty to release Him onto this man. We came to a complete halt as I swung around the bed to meet the patient face-to-face. For once, this man was making eye contact, and I was looking into the eyes of a distressed man.

"I'm going to pray for you." I spoke to him.

He could do nothing but stare right between the brim of my glasses. As he blinked, tears began to fall from the surface of his lids. He knew he was in a lot of trouble, and I knew he was in need of a Savior—Jesus, who was beneath my skin.

Father, I pray right now, that every clot, every bit of blood that is pooling within his brain be released in Jesus's name. That this man would be whole, and by your Spirit— the Holy Helper, he would be brought back to normal and live a life for You.

That was it. I just prayed. And his hand gripped mine as we were agreeing that the help of the Holy One, who was working within us, would give him life *fully* once again. I waited as the staff came, took him, and placed him on the MRI table as the doors shut off in the distance.

It was as if everything slowed down—like an episode off *Chicago Fire* where the staff took the critically ill patient off into the distance as I waited like a family member in the background. All I could think about was what was next?

I stood behind the MRI tech as they scanned his brain. "You're not going to find anything in there," I confidently announced to the staff member. You should have seen the look on his face as if he had no idea what I was talking about. He just glanced at me, dumbfounded, and turned right back at the computer screen to finish the scan.

It's hard for people to understand the presence of the Holy Helper. It becomes foreign to them because much of what we perceive as real cannot be scientifically proven or tangibly seen. But just like the Bible states, "The wind blows where it wishes, and you hear the sound of it, but cannot tell where it comes from or where it goes. So is everyone who is born of the Spirit" (John 3:8).

After ten minutes the staff brought the patient back to me. This time the patient appeared to have some sort of response to my appearance. As the bed moved toward me, he reached out with his left hand and grabbed my arm. I looked down in amazement as he was not able to perform this task before.

He was pointing at himself, like something was different. He was able to feel parts of his body again. I smiled with confidence, and his eyes were able to pan back and forth like he was viewing the world for the first time through a new pair of lenses. We made our way back to the room where an entourage of people awaited our arrival.

As the physicians examined him again, they noticed he was getting much of his sensation back. They were amazed at how much he had recovered in such a short time. The patient kept pointing to his wife and then back at me. It was a little embarrassing as if I was someone who was completely out of place.

He started to mumble. His speech was coming back. The doctors felt at this time that we would need to ship him to a more stroke-savvy hospital where he could receive better care. But the man kept pointing at me. His wife began to cry. She was overwhelmed with emotions that she couldn't seem to contain. I wasn't sure if she was crying tears of joy or uncertainty, not knowing what the next step was.

After many people had left the room, and I was alone with his wife, I told her who I was. Not Aaron, the nurse. Not Aaron, a Joplin resident. I told her I was a son of God. As she looked back at me with amazement, I explained to her that I had prayed over her husband and that he was going to be just fine. Overwhelmed with her own thoughts, I handed her a card and told her, "Call me when your husband gets to feeling better." She took the card, and not long after that the ambulance showed up to take him to a bigger hospital to monitor his symptoms. She didn't have much to say, but she gave me a huge hug as a symbol of her thankfulness.

The man came out of the room and shook my hand with his affected, now-working hand, and I gladly bent over to hug him goodbye. "You are going to be alright, my friend. I'll see you soon." I watched the man, his family, and his wife all exit through the ambulance bay.

Later that afternoon I received a call.

"Aaron?" the voice asked.

"Yes, this is he," I replied.

"Hey, it's Claire," she said, "I wanted to give you an update on my husband." I nodded my head and waited for her conclusion: "He is up walking with the nursing staff right now!"

Compressed with the most joy I had ever felt, I'm pretty sure that I leaped to a new vertical height I'd never reached before. Call the Olympic, high-jump coach!

The wife kept thanking me for what I did and for being obedient to what God had asked me to do. I'm not sure if it was something God actually asked me to do or if I was just living out what He has called all of us to do, so I just responded with, "You're welcome."

You see, it doesn't take much to figure out that what happened is nothing short of a miracle. In fact, we are meant to walk in the miraculous. It's just a byproduct of what it means to be a son of God. I did nothing more than believe and expect the Helper to do his thing. The Bible says, "And these signs will follow those who believe. . . ." (Mark 16:17). What signs? Casting out demons, raising the dead, and healing stroke patients! It's what you and I have been called to do, and it's what finding your burn notice is all about.

In order to tap into His presence, we must be obedient to the hopelessness around us. Think of tapping into the Holy Spirit like starting a new job. As funny as that sounds, I'm serious. When you start a new job, you're very nervous because you are not used to your environment or the people around you. But as you continue to get up and go to work, understanding your job, the work becomes more natural, and you get better at it.

The same goes for the Holy Spirit. Unless you practice Him, how do you ever expect to become experienced with Him? Maybe you have felt the urge to pray for an individual at the grocery store? Maybe you have seen someone walking on crutches get out of his car and wondered if you could pray for God to heal him? Try it. What's the worst that can happen? Nothing?

This I know: if I can step outside of my comfortable shell, I will experience a whole new world of possibilities better than inside my shell of comfort. Every day try using the Holy Spirit to touch others around you. It's not hard, but it does take stepping outside your comfort zone. You will fail at times, and other times you will succeed. But I promise you the successful miracles will outweigh a tower of failures. I have prayed and nothing happens. But I have also prayed and seen something happen that's beyond me.

That's just it, it's not really about us. It's about what God wants to do *through* us! All it takes is one small step for man and one giant leap for all of mankind. I'm pretty sure some astronaut made that statement, but it's so true with you and me. If we make one tap in the water with our finger, a ripple effect can happen beyond our surroundings.

On that day, the day a man came in about to lose his life, the Holy Helper showed up. What's even greater, the MRI scan showed no clot on his brain! Can I get an amen?

God loves to touch others through us. It's a part of His nature. Even Jesus made the statement: "Most assuredly, I say to you, he who believes in Me, the works that I do he will do also; and greater *works* than these he will do, because I go to My Father" (John 14:12). Jesus knew He had to leave. Why? So that the Holy Spirit could make His home within us. How come? That we may bring hope to the hopeless and resurrect things that were once dead. Even a man who had no hope was granted the ability to walk again, praising God down the hospital hallway, while the entire staff sat in awe of the works of the Holy Spirit. So good.

Sofa Mart

The disciples understood what it meant to feel defeat. All their money was weighing in on Jesus, and yet, they found themselves in a predicament now that Jesus had been crucified. There was no plan B.

After the death and crucifixion of Christ, the disciples were at a loss for words and really had no other place to go. So, they gathered in an upper room in an old city of Jerusalem on Mount Zion. This was the one place where they had their last meal with Jesus prior to his imprisonment.

But what they didn't know was that they *were* plan B. They were the ones in whom Jesus wanted to impart His Spirit, the Holy Helper. As they waited in despair and prayer, suddenly something shifted in the atmosphere. They heard a sudden sound from heaven, like a rushing *wind*, and it filled the entire room. Sound familiar to my story from before?

What would appear to be a sight show among the people was the first time that divided tongues, as of fire, sat upon them. What was happening? They were being *filled* with the

Holy Spirit! These were not normal encounters: this was a revelation of God's glory now among the people, and with that comes astronomical signs and wonders. When you find your *fire,* you will be *filled* with the Holy Spirit.

My wife and I had journeyed out among the city to shop for new furniture for our house. If you are like any normal guy, this is like pulling teeth without the uncomfortable dentist chair. My wife passionately wanted to go to Sofa Mart for their big annual sale. Have you ever been to Sofa Mart? It's like a mini-mall for just furniture. You have got to be kidding me! But I, being the great husband that I am, willingly loaded up the vehicle and headed toward this furniture frenzy.

It happened to be raining on this day, so my wife ran in as I gathered the baby from the back seat. Don't worry. I'm bald so it doesn't make a difference if my hair gets wet. As I made my way through the front doors, my wife was already being chatty Cathy with some locals. Or should I say these people were not locals. They were from New Zealand.

The man was fairly tall and slender, and his wife was petite. To me, they didn't look like they matched very well. The man was very personable. He could have talked your head off at a conference, and you wouldn't even have to pay him.

He spoke about America and how much we were in a financial crisis. I almost called him Captain Obvious, but I restrained my tongue. He wanted me to watch a YouTube video that explains the background on how we came to such a corruptible situation. I love YouTube, but I hate politics.

Nevertheless, I obliged him by writing down the video's website.

Not long after that exchange, he kept speaking. (Yes, he was still going.) I knew the conversation was taking a turn and felt the presence of the Holy Helper becoming more apparent. I had to ask him, "Sir, I have to ask you, what is it that you believe?" He stopped frankly in his speech and responded, "Well, I believe in a higher power. I believe that when you die, based on your actions here, you will go to your appropriate destination."

"Cool!" I responded.

You would have thought I had have told him he was all wrong, that he needed to change his ways, or had slapped him upside his head. But I didn't. Instead, I told him what I believed.

"Here's what I believe," I responded. "I believe that Jesus is the Son of God and that He came as fully man and fully God. He died for my sins and was resurrected after the third day. Because of Jesus's love, I now am able to have a relationship with my Father who is in heaven and now the Holy Spirit lives within me."

Before he could even respond, I gently placed my hand on his left shoulder. "Ouch!" he shouted.

I paused as I took in what was actually happening. And then I did it again. I reached over and touched his left shoulder. He flinched even harder this time. Suddenly, this man's thoughts were filled with doubt. What he was actually feeling was the Spirit of God resting among His people, and with that kind of glory, there is no room for argument.

I knew then it was time to show Him the Father, and I asked him if I could pray for him. He kept panning between me and his wife with no other choice but to say yes. So, we prayed, and I felt the room shift. Just like when the disciples were in the upper room, waiting and watching, this man received the Father's love for the first time.

After we had finished praying, I opened my eyes, and the man was sobbing. He couldn't even look me in the eyes. He hugged my wife, bypassed his, and exited the Sofa Mart. As his wife went to chase him out the door, she stopped. And suddenly she turned to us, "Thank you so much. You have no idea how much he needed that." Then we saw them drive off in the distance.

You may be asking yourself what just happened? I sure did. What actually happened was that this was a man, who never knew what it was like to experience God, and suddenly, in the middle of a Sofa Mart on a Saturday morning, he had the privilege to witness the reality of heaven and what that felt like. My wife and I could hardly ever shop for furniture, but we were both wrecked by what had just happened. I felt waves of ambience from the Holy Spirit.

I don't know what happened to that man and his wife. I don't have to. All I had to do was be a resting place for the Holy Helper. He would handle the rest. This I know: if you would be willing to allow the Holy Spirit to move effortlessly through you and never allow fear to get the best of you, miraculous things can happen.

The disciples were now on a new journey in their lives once they were touched by the Holy Helper. You may say they actually were just beginning their first burn notice because the fire of God was exploding deep within their souls. They were recognizing their God-given purpose now and that the Navigator, who once walked with them and was crucified, was now going to be the navigational unit *within* them.

That's just it, when the Holy Spirit makes His mark within you, waves of opportunity will follow. The disciples headed out on their journey with a new Friend. They would be closely united. Everything in their past—their failures, doubts, uncertainty, and loss—would be accumulated into one extraordinary journey. It was time that they carried out their burn notice.

Marching Orders

The Holy Spirit is available at all times. Jesus told the disciples, "For John truly baptized with water, but you shall be baptized with the Holy Spirit not many days from now" (Acts 1:5). The same is true today. I want you to test the waters. As you are walking in the grocery store, at the mall, in the marketplace, at school, or within the community, find people who may need prayer. Ask God to use you for His glory and watch your journey come to life. Just like a new job, you may be a little off at first, but over time you will begin to build experience and hear and see things clearer. Don't let fear evaporate your untouchable faith. "There is no fear in love; but perfect love casts out fear" (1 John 4:18). Allow the Holy Helper to be your guide.

CHAPTER 7:

The Burning Bush

had finally made my way home from an exhilarating
weekend in Kansas City. We had spent numerous days
soaking up the worship music, practical teachings, and
closeness with the body of Christ. If you had never made
your way to *Onething* put on by IHOP (International House
of Prayer), I dare you to go.

My wife and I had packed our luggage in the back of our
vehicle and headed on our way home. We were like little
schoolgirls chatting it up in the front seat with the residue
of joy fermented deep within our hearts from the event. To

much of my surprise, I didn't know leaving a conference would bring so much separation anxiety, but it did.

We had made our way through the front door of our home, and suddenly, I caught myself alone, staring down at the floor of my walk-in closet as I dropped my backpack off my shoulder. It was one of those moments like when you were watching a movie and the actor either made a really bad decision and everything was in slow-mow or the actor was on the brink of a life changing epiphany. Either way, something was churning deep inside of me.

Is this it? I'm just going to go back to my normal, everyday life? I thought. What I had experienced back at *Onething* was a glimpse of heaven, and I wanted more of it. I wanted to feel the waves of emotion carry swiftly over my body as I plunged under the trough of the ocean. Simply put: I knew there was a calling on my life, and I had to find out what it was.

Moses was a man who had much anointing on his life. Even from birth, he was saved from the Egyptian armies. Pushed down the Nile River by his parents, he was moved into the arms of the ones who attempted to kill every boy from Israel in the first place. But he wasn't killed, and he was cared for by Pharaoh's daughter herself.

As Moses grew up, he was caught in a conflict between two men, and he killed an Egyptian. To help him avoid the death penalty, he fled Egypt and was on the run from Pharaoh. And this is the moment *everything* changed for Moses, when he was sideswiped by a burning bush.

Now, I don't know about you, but if I saw a burning bush, I would have either called the fire department or attempted to look the other way, hoping someone else would handle the problem. That's just me.

One thing that caught Moses's eye was the bush wouldn't burn up. It was an inferno with no extinguisher. Personally, I would have hoped he had some fire training. Then a voice came, "Moses! Moses!" (Exodus 3:4). And Moses responded, "Here I am" (Exodus 3:4). It was the first encounter Moses ever had with God, and it was the first phase of Moses's new revelation. It was Moses's burn notice, literally.

When God calls you, everything changes—your thoughts, your desires, your path, even your life. It's your one moment where you find yourself staring at the floor of your closet thinking, *Is this it? I know there's more.* You can't help but fall into the arms of the One who holds your life in the first place. After all, you and I were created for a purpose.

Moses's entire journey would be detoured by a burning shrub. But everything leading up to Moses life is significant—from the basket floating down the river, to the escape from the Egyptians, and everything in between. This was just the beginning of what would be an extraordinary life designed by an extraordinary God. That's all Moses needed, one bush blazing in the sunset, to recognize that his life was meant for so much more.

From Poverty to Pastries

One of my good friends, Mickel Clark, is a man with a big heart. Though his outgoing personality outweighs any competition, Mickel came from a house of brokenness. As a child, he grew up in a fatherless home. His mother desperately found herself playing both roles.

At age nine, Mickel and his mother moved to Joplin where they would be overcome with poverty and more broken relationships. Mickel started attending the local Boys & Girls Club where he met some pretty outstanding role models who took him under their wing. In time, Mikel would attend church, and by age fourteen, he knew there was a calling by God for his life.

He no longer had to worry about where his next meal would come from nor if he would have a roof over his head. He didn't have to fantasize about what a father represented, for he was experiencing the true Father of heaven. In a sense, he was leaving the stereotypical category of every other person who had destined him for failure because of his past, being a poor boy in a fatherless home.

Mikel's life changed drastically over the years. He fell in love with his sweetheart, and by 2012 they were married. As Mikel aged he became involved in the youth at church. Mikel and his wife grew hungry to become parents. But after many attempts, they found themselves still childless. Then one day their pastor's wife approached them with some strange news. There were two boys who desperately needed a family to love them. The boys were on the brink of being placed in the foster system forever if they didn't find a permanent placement immediately.

Due to circumstances, the state had gotten involved and were looking for placement. Mikel and his wife, at first, didn't think much of it. They were wanting their own children. But something was burning deep within their hearts that could not be hidden: parenthood. So, they prayed and waited for their answer.

It wouldn't take long before they got a phone call by a social worker one day. You see, it takes a lot of time and preparation to become a foster parent—classes, house monitoring, and the works. It can take months before you get approved. But not when God's hand is in the mix, then doors just begin to open.

The social worker wanted Mikel and his wife for these boys. He told them that there was an emergency placement program where the normal process could be waived and they could obtain a license immediately. How cool! But the Clarks had to make a decision: would they take a step of faith toward obtaining these boys and giving them something they never had before, or would they decline the offer and go back to trying for their own children?

Mikel seemingly recalled a moment when he was with me in Brazil where one of the other youth leaders spoke into his life. He told Mikel this, "You can go back to what you know, or you can trust God with the unknown." Likewise, Mikel seemed to remind me of something I had said to him during the same time period, "God will never give you your 'yes' or your 'no'—otherwise, we would never explore our faith in Him. It's when we travel into the *unknown* that we will be given our answer."

This is a good spot for this: unless you travel into the most unknown areas of your life, you will never understand the true nature of God. He looks for individuals who will trust Him and will say "yes," even when it doesn't make sense, or who will be okay with the "no" after we have failed. Faith is not an option: it's a requirement.

If you ever expect to find your burn notice, you will have to take a chance. For Mikel, all it would take was his "yes," and God would do the rest. So, they did it. They became parents in an instant, with no regrets, and jumped into this gigantic pool of hope. Cannonball! They knew there was a higher calling on their lives—higher than just being parents. They were given the opportunity to love others more than themselves. Not only would these two boys come to know love through Mikel and his wife, but they would become a huge piece to this family's puzzle.

The two boys were inseparable from the Clarks. In due time, the Clarks would not only go on to foster these two boys, but also they adopted them into their family! Being a family of four, you would have assumed they'd call it quits, but then one of the adopted boys had a dream.

"Daddy, I dreamed that we had a sister." the boy spoke. Mikel, thrown off by his response, really thought nothing of it until one day when they were sitting in their house with an extra bedroom and he heard the audible voice of God, "Why are you not filling this room with my children?" That changed everything.

Mikel's wife even was having vivid dreams of a girl. Then they got an unexpected phone call, again. It was their social worker, and he had some more strange news. The sister of their two adopted boys had been born and potentially was going to be turned over to the state. Once again, the Clarks had to make a decision about whether they would take another child into their home.

As you would assume, the doors blew wide open, and the Clarks were blessed with a beautiful baby girl. Now, they were a family of five, and Mikel and his wife were outnumbered. They moved from man-to-man coverage to zone play!

You have to understand the significance of this story. Mikel, a boy who would be categorized to fail because of his past, was moving on to greater things. Though he was fatherless as a child, he had a passion to become a father to the fatherless. It was his burn notice. He desperately wanted to give others what he lacked. This I know: what you lack in your life, through trials and tribulations, is the very thing that God wants to fill.

Burn notice is taking what you are passionate about, recognizing it, and inserting it into your life. You have to go after it like it was a part of you. It will never be easily handed over to you, but you need to explore it. But all it takes is desire—*I know there's more.*

Moses was destined to die. Killed by the Egyptians because of his gender, he was pushed down the river. Low and behold, he escaped obstacle after obstacle. And then one day, when he least expected it, God would appear through a burning bush and set his life on a trajectory of purpose.

But the story with Mikel didn't stop there. Not only did he have a passion to become a parent, he had a passion for culinary art. He had been working some dead-end jobs along with some average restaurant positions, but Mikel's passion was to become a chef.

After the Clarks became a family of five, he started slinging some meat and inviting people over to try out his recipes from his back yard. Over time, Mikel's food became a sensation. He knew it was time to find a kitchen.

This I know: when you are passionate about what God is passionate about, He will eventually give you your desires. For Mikel, he took these abandoned children into his home, and generously God gave him a kitchen. It would become his own home away from home.

Mikel's business flourished, becoming one of the best catering companies in the city. Clark's Catering LLC was established, and now Mikel is able to live out his dream—both dreams that is: being a father and being a chef. How cool is that?

The same goes for your story. There is an inferno resting deep within your soul, and in order to ignite the match, you have to have passion. Once the passion is put in its place, there is no other area for your life to go than to burn. Burn to reach new heights. Burn to be a glory piece for the kingdom as if you were created for so much more.

Don't sell yourself short by waiting. "Now when He was asked by the Pharisees when the kingdom of God would come, He answered them and said, 'The kingdom of God does not come with observation; nor will they say, "See here!" or "See there!" For indeed, the kingdom of God is within you'" (Luke 17:20–21). In this, we also know that, "For our God is a consuming fire" (Hebrews 12:29). This is revelation: that we would understand the magnitude of heaven within us and have the ability to burn as a consuming fire—igniting, displaying, engulfing everything around us, and, ultimately, changing our own environments.

Moses knew his life had taken on new meaning. Once God told Moses to go back to Pharaoh in order to bring the Israelites out of slavery, he would face many obstacles and trials, such as keeping the Israelites positive, preventing them from worshipping other gods, and running from the Egyptian army. It's not always easy to follow your burn notice, and you will get singed once in a while. But just on the other side of resistance is a world of opportunity.

Moses and the Israelites found themselves stuck on the edge of the shore of the Red Sea. The Israelites were terrified, crying out to God and cussing out Moses. But Moses responded with three of the most powerful words, "Don't. Be. Afraid!"

You may be on the shore of distress right now. You may be on the brink of a breakdown, wondering how will I overcome this obstacle? But I assure you that God fights your every battle. Use these three words that will help you overcome your fear: "Don't be afraid!"

Fear does nothing more than attempt to bring us back to our original position. It places thoughts in our heads that say, *We can't accomplish this. We'll never escape. I don't see a way out.* The Lord fights for you. You need not to be afraid. Even with an Egyptian army at the back of Moses, he knew he was living his burn notice, and it was up to his faith to finish what God had already started.

"And Moses said to the people, 'Do not be afraid. Stand still, see the salvation of the LORD, which He will accomplish for you today. For the Egyptians again whom you see today, you shall see again no more forever. The LORD will fight for you, and you shall hold your peace'" (Exodus 14:13–14). The tone or faith in Moses's voice would shift the atmosphere as God would command him to strike his walking stick into the water. So, Moses held out his hand over the sea, and the walls of the waters would begin to swell and separate.

Your faith snuffs out your fears. When you stand your ground, God will sustain His promise. Strike the ground! Stand tall and be not afraid. For God goes with you wherever you are. Burn like never before. Burn with desire because right at the time when the pressure of your fears begin to swell, the power of God will show you the way out. Actually, He will part the waters of your Red Sea, giving you faith like never before. Know this: you will never know the *size* of your faith until you *step* out in faith, knowing it was faith that got you there.

My burn notice started in the middle of my closet, looking at the ground, knowing there was so much more for my life. This would move me to hear the voice of God in the middle of church that would say, "I need you outside these four walls." I would go on to explore what that meant for my life.

God will never give you the whole picture. He will only give you a portion of it. If you expect things to just show up on your front porch, you will be mistakenly disappointed. I agree there are times of waiting, but I believe there are more instances of wonder where we find out what we were created for in the first place.

Where are you at right now? What do you feel God is speaking in this very moment? He may have placed something on your heart, and you just haven't jumped. I would encourage you to jump. Burn notice is not about going through the motions and hoping one day something happens, it's *expecting* something to happen as we go through the motions.

For me, it's recognizing the hand of God in my life and obeying the instructions He gives me. It's letting go of what I feel or what I want. I feel lots of things, but I know the calling on my life. I could sum it up with this sentence: to know there's always more by exploring my surroundings and going after the God who calms the waves and is the Author and Finisher of my life.

Once you understand the significance of your life, it's time to go out and create waves of opportunity. Like Moses said to the Israelites, "Don't be afraid!" and then the Red Sea parted to what would become one of the greatest miracles of all time. All he had to do was walk.

Marching Orders

Throughout this chapter you have stepped foot into what burn notice accumulates. It takes you to new levels, different heights, reckless faith, and ultimately your calling. Everyone has a calling. I like to call it your personal imprint in this world. But it must be explored. Your burn notice can be an encounter with God, a repetitive thought, or an overwhelming passion for something. Whatever it looks like, explore it. Go after it. Remember, it won't just sit and wait for you, but you must embrace it. Burn like never before and just see where God will take you next.

CHAPTER 8:

Creating Opportunity

S.O.S. Ministries had left its imprint in the community. It was being known for its generosity as well as its authenticity. It's funny when you hear about reviews on Google for a business or organization where people emphasize their perspective about something, but for me, my reviews came from the Lord. He would have given us a five-star review with an endorsement of His goodness. Why? Because what we were doing was serving others and giving ourselves up for a friend. We were becoming the model for what Jesus would preach to the people. But what's even more insurmountable is that we were creating a stage of opportunity, not just for the people we served but also for the community that served alongside us.

I'm an opportunist by nature. I always feel deep down in my bones that there's more. Like urgency, I can't seem to sit still. It might be my ADD (attention-deficit disorder) running wild, but I truly go after the invisible, as though the characteristics of heaven are upon me.

The disciples knew what it meant to be opportunists. I mean, they walked with the Man who walked on water, who showed them miracles, signs, and wonders, washed their feet, and ultimately showed them the way to life. Who couldn't have urgency after that?

Once the Holy Spirit had breathed upon them in the upper room, it was time. No longer would they doubt about what the next step was. All they had to do was step because now the Spirit who lived inside them was greater than anything of this world. The church would become mobile, and it would spread like wildfire!

Not long after Peter had been baptized with the Holy Spirit and his entourage was speaking in many different tongues, the people around them thought they were drunk. Come on guys, it's 10:00 a.m. But Peter stood with authority because he had something different flowing through his veins: "Then Peter said to them, 'Repent, and let every one of you be baptized in the name of Jesus Christ for the remission of sins; and you shall receive the gift of the Holy Spirit" (Acts 2:38).

Peter was waving what he had onto others. He, in a sense, was creating opportunity for others by what he already carried. And low and behold, immediately 3,000 souls were added to the kingdom that day. Now that's what I call opportunity!

It didn't take Peter and his men long to understand: they were living out their burn notice, and the explosion of increase rested upon their souls. They journeyed out, in their sandals, and became mobile. Their first case of faith would be a doozy. They met a man who was paralyzed from birth at a gate called Beautiful. How odd.

Daily this man would be laid at the gate to beg for money and food. Every day he waited, hoping that someone would give him a bit more change than the yesterday, and yet, every day not once did he feel his life would change. But when the Spirit who is on the move shows up at a gate called Beautiful, there would be no other choice but for a miraculous encounter to happen. Peter and John would approach this gate, and here would be their first opportunity.

As the man reached out with his hand in a begging manner the disciples responded: "And fixing his eyes on him, with John, Peter said, 'Look at us'" (Acts 3:4). Expecting to receive something—a denarius, loaf of bread, the clothes on their backs, string cheese, anything—"Peter said, 'Silver and gold I do not have, but what I do have I give you: In the name of Jesus Christ of Nazareth, rise up and walk'" (Acts 3:6).

Peter took him by the right hand, lifted him up, and immediately he was mobile. Such opportunity! The man took off leaping, running, and praising God in the temple alongside Peter and John. Not only did the miracle affect the man lying at the gate, but it also affected every eye that witnessed this within the temple. It was the opportunity the disciples had received in the upper room, where a man would receive the same opportunity to walk again, contagiously affecting the people in the temple who would witness this massive opportunity. It was like a domino effect.

I have experienced a similar case of my gate called beautiful. A man, who was homeless, was known in the community as a traveler. Clothed with his iconic grey jacket, oversized duffle bag, and frayed jeans, he would show up all over the city in different areas. Unfortunately, it was very difficult to get near this man because he suffered from mental illness.

One day, I had stopped at the post office to drop off some mail. I had approached the side door as I looked down at my feet to see this same man sitting at the foundation of the building near the entrance. The entrance I would call beautiful.

I approached the man and asked probably what no one had asked him before, "What's your name?" I could have asked him about his past, his current living conditions, or what he was doing out here in the heat in front of the post office, but I didn't. I wanted to know *who* he was.

I think we get a lot of things wrong. We assume everyone is needing something when, in reality, most people just want to be known. Perhaps it's the child-like character inside me, but I think getting to know people is the most powerful tool of humanity that anyone can carry.

The man paused, and you could tell he was mentally struggling. I asked him again, "What's your name?" His lips were quivering. His hands began to fidget. I could tell this man had little to no communication with people.

After he didn't respond for some time, I asked him then if he was hungry. He quickly shook his head yes. So, I asked him if we could go have lunch, but I'm pretty sure that was like asking him if he wanted to go skydiving out of the side of a plane without a parachute—not going to happen.

I reached down into my wallet and pulled out a twenty-dollar bill. "Here, I want you to have this to get something to eat." The man had reached out just like the beggar at the gate called Beautiful as I gently laid the money in his hand.

"My name is Larry," the man softly said.

Wow! He has a name. His name is Larry. I bet never in his current situation had anyone asked him his name. For me, this was a breakthrough. I wasn't after his possessions—he had none—or his recognition. I was after his *name*.

Jesus was a man after men. He never wanted their possessions, their treasure, or their recognition. He wanted their *name*. Why? Because what He represented was love, and with love comes intimate relationship.

That's the thing, God wants to know you as well. He wants to know your name, your heart, and everything you desire. You're His desire, and He never leaves any of His children unattended because He is with them wherever they go.

You may have had some pretty hard experiences where you didn't feel the presence of God. For Larry, he suffered from mental illness. For him, he probably never felt the hand of God through the voices rattling around in his head. But for some reason, on this day, God would use me to encounter him and ask him his name. It was opportunity.

There are people all around you who are begging for an opportunity—a window crease of hope. They may have been praying to God, asking God to save them and the situation they are in. But so far, they have received no answer . . . until the day when you could be the answer they have been asking for all along.

After Larry had given me his name, I asked if I could pray for him. Unfortunately, he was not a personable individual, so he declined. That doesn't matter. What matters is that I showed my compassion for him by asking his name. God will do the rest.

I had made my way into the post office to make my purchase and turned to leave the facility. As I left the building, anticipating Larry was gone, he was still sitting stationary with his hand out and the twenty-dollar bill still resting in his hand.

"That's for you, Larry," I said with urgency, "I want you to have it."

From Larry's response, I assumed that no one had showed him kindness like this before and that he had no idea about how to respond. So, he just kept his hand out as if I wanted it back.

People all around you have no clue on how to respond when you show them kindness. It's abnormal according to humanity. But when Jesus showed up in a certain environment with one thing on his mind—compassion, people were moved from closed off to opened up.

I love Larry, and I don't even know him. But I want to. God wants to know him. And if I am any image of God, then the two just line up. If we are going to create opportunity around us, we must open up and give our lives to the calling of God. And at just the right moment, when nothing seems to happen, He will place a Larry in your path who is desperately in need of love because He has called you to be compassionate for the least of these. Larry was forever changed this day as he drifted off into the sunset with a duffle bag over his shoulder and a fresh, crisp twenty-dollar bill.

Where Do We Go from Here?

After we heard word that the Salvage Yard would be closing, we were homeless. It's ironic thinking back to when S.O.S. Ministries was an organization that was homeless, feeding the homeless. I chuckle at it now. But we had fuel. We had received a check in the mail that gave us hope, knowing there was more to the equation. We just didn't have the answer yet.

We had made many attempts to find a new home. We tried to serve inside churches and community centers, being shut down by city organizations and left feeling like something was missing. It can be difficult when you know and understand the hand of God in your life and then you are abruptly left confused. *What now? Everything was moving in the right direction. Where do we go from here?*

Then suddenly, I heard from the Lord, "It's time to go back to where you started." To me, this didn't make sense. Lots of things do not make sense when walking the narrow path, but I had instructions. It's was time to go back to the park.

Any time we moved to a new location it would take approximately two to four weeks to get the people back. We had anticipated the numbers to be low when we showed up that next week, but something was off. There were more people there than when we originally started!

Actually, we started hitting an all-time high. There was something about the streets that made these people comfortable, and to them this was their church building. We had different churches serving alongside us, but we needed more. Quickly word got out that we were back serving the streets, and churches started to call.

This is where opportunity hits its peak: not only were we serving the people, giving them an opportunity to be loved, but we had created an environment for churches, giving them the opportunity to serve as well. So, in essence, it was an epicenter of opportunity. To me, it was the kingdom of God.

This is a good point here: creating opportunity is nothing more than discipleship, giving people the same authority you have to utilize their gifts and calling, and giving people ownership. It doesn't take much—just a window of opportunity that ultimately releases great possibility. To me, this was home. I was finding myself in a place of peace and contentment. This I know: if you are functioning in your calling, it just becomes easy. Not that you won't hit road bumps along the way, but it's where you find your sweet spot and where what you do becomes instinctive.

The disciples were homeless. They were without walls. Yet they began to see and hear with a new Spirit. The kingdom of God is never about an internal consumption, hoarding the gospel for ourselves, but it was more of an outward combustion. Essentially, the kingdom of God is an overflowing drench of opportunity.

In the book of Acts, it was the beginning of what would be called "the church." But it took bold moves, being chased by the Roman empire, falsely imprisoned, being denied more times than they could count, and lacking clothing, food, or any place of residence. It didn't matter to them: they were living out their burn notice.

Missed Opportunity

When I was finishing my master's degree, I had been working in the ER for years. I had made my career there. Though deep down inside I wanted to work there when I finished school, the job didn't line up. But working in the ER left a lot of room for decisions. I was surrounded by general surgeons, internal medicine physicians, hospice, psychologists, and cardiologists.

There was one specialty that stuck out to me the most, orthopedic medicine. Even more, there was a certain surgeon whom I looked up to. I said, "That is who I would love to work for." Little did I know that one day I would get a phone call.

"Are you looking for a job?" he asked.

Surprised by the phone call, I was silenced for a moment. "Yes, I'm looking for a job," I softly replied.

I mean, come on. You go to school to get a job, right? For being a surgeon, he didn't appear to have a lot of common sense (sarcasm inserted here). So, I was taken out to dinner and given the opportunity to partner with one of the best orthopedic surgeons in the area.

Something else happened though. It was like my life was opened up into a telemarketing company because I started getting phone calls from all different specialties. The hospital I worked for actually sat me down for a meeting and gave me a pamphlet of areas they wanted me to work. I had general surgeons calling me, primary care doctors, and everything in between.

Was this really happening? I haven't even graduated yet, and opportunity seems to be knocking at my door. I was honored that so many doctors wanted me for their team. That's the thing, when you are in the righteousness of God, opportunity always seems to find you. I'm all for opportunity, but this was ridiculous.

After much prayer, I didn't get an answer. Sometimes it's not about how much you pray but about where your desire is. The Bible says, "Delight yourself also in the LORD, And He shall give you the desires of your heart" (Psalm 37:4). Well, I was so much in love with God that delight became my middle name.

For me, my desire was to work for the orthopedic surgeon, pushing aside all other opportunities. I took the job, and, little did I know, it would be the most difficult path for my life.

My first day had come, and I was introduced to many collaborative staff in many different environments. There were days we were in the clinic, and other days we were inserted into multiple different areas in the operating room. It's funny looking back at me being the new guy, attempting to don gloves and put on my surgical uniform. I broke sterile field so many times that I took gowns home to practice. Pathetic.

The thing about surgery is that you are surrounded by the most socially accepted surgeons. I found myself in a lions' den of high-paid medical representatives, anesthesiologists, and, of course, an army of surgeons. I even dined daily with the hospital board and CEOs.

From many people's perspective, I was living the "successful" life. I had made it big, invited into the homes of billion-dollar company owners, surrounded by exotic cars, and holding conversations with state representatives. You could say I was living the America dream.

But this wasn't a dream, but rather it was a nightmare. I found myself both mentally and physically exhausted. We would strenuously work sixteen hours in the surgery room multiple times a week. I was always away from my family, which put more stress on my wife. I had no orthopedic background, so I had to learn a new language all together. And on top of that, there was no one to train me, and I was like a lost sheep among wolves.

I had signed a contract, so I was in it for the long haul. After the months went by, I felt trapped, like there was literally no way out. Needless to say, my prayer life increased. I found myself outside the hospital talking with God to give me the strength and the endurance to get through another day. Even on my days off, I was getting phone calls from the hospital. It appeared that my phone was on a timed dial because I was getting phones calls every hour. I seemed to be drifting off away from my family and ministry as the months flew by.

Opportunity is a great thing. You can feel the movement of the door open up and yet find yourself in an environment that you didn't intend to be on the other side of. For me, it was treacherous. I became hopeless. Stress became my second nature.

I loved my surgeon. We got along great. It wasn't our relationship that was the problem, it was the workload. And, to me, it didn't feel like my burn notice. There will be times in your life that you may fall off the path God intended for you. It can leave you discouraged, discontent, and depressed. But always remember this, "A man's heart plans his way, But the Lord directs his steps" (Proverbs 16:9).

So, for me, I had made my plans by taking the job. But to be honest with you, I did grow closer to God and my wife during the process. The Lord tests our hearts. He wants to know during the most difficult times if you will you trust Him. Will you call on Him? Will you give your life as a ransom for Him?

My prayer life was on fire. My relationship with my wife grew deeper. Emily was such a supporter for me and a prayer advocate while I worked. I felt the overwhelming presence of God while I grinded through my day and was able to touch the lives of others around me. I took what was difficult and made it my learning lesson. It was stretching me for greatness!

Statistics say that the average person meets three new people every day. That's an average of 1,000 people per year. If the average person goes on to live eighty years, that's 80,000 people in our lifetime—enough to fill London's Olympic Stadium!

As people walking out our burn notice, we should be encountering people every day. Something that I am assessing in our society is how we are becoming so disconnected that we are missing opportunities. We're often capsized by social media, isolation, and too busy running our own lives to give others our time. Missed opportunities leave people outside the kingdom of God.

Jesus was really good about creating opportunity. He would show up to funerals and stand against impossible situations, even when hanging on the cross at Calvary, He extended opportunity to a man who would presumably perish. "And Jesus said to him, 'Assuredly, I say to you, today you will be with Me in paradise'" (Luke 23:43), as the man displayed his faith in Jesus. That's opportunity even to the brink of death.

Opportunity is being open. It's allowing people to sit in your living room and telling them about the miraculous hand of God in your life. It's pulling over to someone whose car has broken down and lending a hand. Basically, it's giving up your life for others so that they may experience and witness God through your good works.

Prayer should become our first language. Pray daily that God would give you opportunities to display His love to others. It's not difficult: it's simple. In fact, simplicity *is* the gospel. Paul warned us about making things too complicated. He said, "But I fear, lest somehow, as the serpent deceived Eve by his craftiness, so your minds may be corrupted from the simplicity that is in Christ" (2 Corinthians 11:3).

I'm afraid we have made things so complicated that we have blocked the gospel from getting into the laps of the lost. Don't be so narrow minded that you are no longer earthly available. Give, love, and go after the people whom Jesus died for. Make opportunity become a badge of honor. We are merely men without Christ, but men who are ordained by the hand of God—now that's an entirely different story.

Don't miss it. Don't be sideswiped by the cunning craft of the devil. He is not intimidated by church attendance, Bible studies, or anything else on our Christian lists. He is intimidated by the bold and courageous move of God's children who save those who are hopeless and in need of a Savior. Those people frighten him because they are increasing the kingdom of God.

I had made a pretty poor decision by taking on the new job, but God was faithful in getting me through the most difficult situations and granting me peace along the way. Eventually, I left the practice but learned a lot during my time there. Opportunity can be appealing, but sometimes it's not the right path He has for you. It can become missed opportunity. Thank God that He places one foot in front of another as I continue to seek Him in everything I do. Getting me on the right path and back to what I was designed to do—now that's what I call opportunity!

Marching Orders

Opportunity is one of the greatest things in the kingdom. God sets them up, and we knock them down. I want you to pray to God and ask Him to give you opportunity and then go look for it. It can be in the marketplace, at the mall, or at a convenient store. It doesn't matter where, but just be open about your faith. If you miss it, don't dwell on it, but learn from what you have experienced and move forward. Start a movement centered around passion and fuel others around you to want to jump on board. That is opportunity, not just in your life but in others. Go be an opportunist who shows up in the middle of the crowd and screams, "Follow me, it's this way to opportunity!" The people will surely follow.

CHAPTER 9:

Risk Takers

Robert "Evel" Knievel was known as one of the greatest daredevils of all time. He could reach the highest ascents brought forth by some of the wickedest defeats. He wore a cap, strapped steel-toe boots, and maybe a signature helmet, if he was in the mood. He often is quoted for saying, "Kids wanted to be like me, men wanted to be me, and the women wanted to be with me."[1]

At age eight he was inspired after attending a Joie Chitwood Auto Daredevil Show, to which he later gave credit for his career choice based on his fanatic interest in the extremist lifestyle of this man.[2] After that, he started racing motorcycles in mining-scarred landscapes with his bicycle at an early age and would later realize this was the calling for his life.

In the waking moments of January 23, 1966, Knievel would perform wheelies, crash through plywood firewalls, and jump over two pickup trucks. The show became a success overnight! He was asked to host many more shows in the near future.

Evel Knievel didn't continue to be successful because he had many defeats and many broken bones. He's actually in the *Guinness Book of World Records* for the most broken bones—433 to be exact.[3] I don't know if I would call that an endeavor or not, but hey, if the shoe fits.

While people were jumping pools, Knievel was jumping fleets of trucks. When most people would have stopped, Evel kept adding more cars, more fiery rings, more obstacles, and longer distances. Basically, everything incorporated as impossible, Knievel embraced.

Much of his fame would come from a night when he jumped Caesar's Palace fountains in Las Vegas, Nevada. ABC declined his offer to televise the event but did speculate that they would air it if he took his own video and sent it in at a later date.

With all bets against him, he came up short, crushing his pelvis and femur. Little did Knievel know that this crash would be the turning point he needed. ABC aired it, and it became a sensation. The doctors told him he would more than likely never walk again without crutches—let alone ride a motorcycle. This crash would go down in the books as the most famous crash in history, and it would inspire him to go on to jump the Grand Canyon, jump the Snake River Canyon, and leap over a death-defying fourteen Greyhound buses.[4]

There is no doubt that Evel Knievel was living out his burn notice. He took what was impossible and made it possible. The passion that burned deep with inside him could not be snuffed out by anyone—not the media and not the cynics closest to him. It was just him, his trusty bike, and a whole lot of courage.

That's the thing: Knievel defined death. He went after it every day, not to embrace it but to beat it. He showed the world that through one idea, he could set in motion the delusional paralysis that prevents us from our calling. Simply put: he showed fear that it had no hold on him. When we don't follow through with our passions, our lives become, well, motionless. But if I could sum up Kneivel's life in one word, it wouldn't be his talent or his mindset. People didn't identify him for that, but they identified him for his *risk*.

We can learn a lot from Knievel. If we would push past our fears and believe, just believe, that on the other side of faith is a world full in motion, never motionless. When we are paralyzed by our fears, it prevents us from our purpose. Was Knievel scared? You bet. But it didn't paralyze him, but rather it motivated him because he saw a world of endless opportunity just on the other side of the ramp. Every landing was a celebration, giving the world an illustration of what overcoming looks like. And overcame he did!

For you and me, the lesson here is the same. You may be looking at your situation now, wondering how you will overcome your fear. We can either feed the fear or know through faith that fear is a liar. It's ultimately our choice. But in order to step foot into our burn notice, we are going to have to take courage, and above all, at some point, we're going to have to take risk.

4,000 Emails

I had my roots deep within the soil at the emergency department. I had made many moves from different jobs to get me where I was now. I loved the ER. I loved how unstable it was. Even though that sounds brainwashed, I enjoyed a good cup of chaos. After all, I'm a box of assorted crayons myself.

The ER was a place that acquired bad attitudes. Rightly so, we dealt with people who would spit on us, hit us, and say some of the most inhuman things. Negativity can grow on you. It can begin to consume you. Jesus never said, "Love just the people who love you back." Rather, He said, "But I say to you who hear: Love your enemies, do good to those who hate you, bless those who curse you, and pray for those who spitefully use you" (Luke 6:27–28). So, I take what Jesus tells me, and I run with it. Sometimes running can get you into a whole lot of trouble.

Overwhelmed by all the negativity happening around me, I found myself sitting in front of a computer at work. I thought to myself, *What if I could release positivity into the staff and ultimately change the environment around me?* So, I pulled up my email and started to write.

It was a Monday. Every human on planet earth hates Mondays. I guess it's the thought of going back to reality that really irks some people. But I wanted to flip the script. I love encouraging people, and I figured what better way than to send out a mass email to all my fellow coworkers? Not just to the ER staff but to 4,000 people inside a health system.

It was a short, two-paragraph letter. Do you know what I titled it? "Case of the Mondays." Genius! I figured with so much stigma surrounding Mondays, what if we made this Monday one of the best yet? As I finished the blog, I hit send. I had no idea what response I would get.

I had gone back to my job and continued to care for the sick. In and out of rooms, I was starting IVs, dispensing medication, and documenting cases. Then, suddenly, I would hear the first comment.

"Love what you wrote, Aaron," the staff mentioned. Being the inattentive person that I am, I didn't have a clue what they were saying until it dawned on me, *Oh yeah, the emails!*

I raced back to my computer and jumped into my seat at the desk and had no idea what I would witness. Over the day hundreds of people responded. Testimonies of how much the message brought happiness to their jobs and hope within their hearts. Evidently, what was happening is that I was taking a huge risk and seeing lives changed all around the health system.

You never know what one drop of water in a large pond can create. Risk doesn't take much energy, but it takes a large amount of risk to create a wavelength of change. Seeing the response from so many people, I knew that I was on to something, so I continued to write.

My messages became fuel to the workers. Like gasoline, I sparked a match, and fires started all over the hospital (not literally, of course). I had people greeting me in the hallway, telling me of certain messages that hit home in their lives. It started to stir up attention, not just from workers who enjoyed the messages but also from others who did not.

After about the third message, I started getting negative feedback. Some people actually asked me to stop emailing them. My boss pulled me aside one day, even though he was a supporter of what I was doing, and he asked me to stop because the higher-ups had instructed him to do so.

Unfortunately, the emails and messages stopped. I want you to know this: anytime there is resistance, just on the other side is a breakthrough. Don't allow what others shut down in your life to be the stopping marker for your calling. Many people get pushed away for doing what is right, but many more people get brought in for their perseverance. This is a good point here: don't stop at failure because those who push past failure set up the courses for their futures. They are the ones who successfully meet their goals and, ultimately, their callings.

Even though I was shut down for writing inspiration all over the hospital, and it wasn't even religious, the people, who needed to see it, saw it. Shortly after I was shut down another email came through, and this time it was administration. But I received a peculiar response.

The administration actually liked what I was putting out there because they saw it as employee satisfaction. What had happened is that many people had emailed the administration and wanted to see more of this on their daily reports. The administration had heard what was said and responded.

My writing within the health system went on to become a daily blog. They actually gave it a catchy title, "Articles by Aaron." Cool, huh? I was living out my burn notice. I love to inspire people and what better way to inspire others than at the place people wish they were not at the most—work.

Risk is cultivating. It takes a certain kind of skill to implement it. It takes a dare devil like Evil Knievel to jump over the Grand Canyon, showing others what is possible, and it takes a nobody like myself to jump across the page toward other coworkers, creating hope in their lives where it once did not live.

If you ever expect to find your burn notice, it will take risk. I will say this: go out and make risk your guide. You don't have to be seat belted in to be safe, and you don't have to stay in the boat any longer. Peter knew what it was like to walk on water. While all the others sat in the boat, Peter took the largest risk of all. All he needed to know was, "Jesus, is that you?" And when he had heard the voice of the One who calms the wind and the storm tell him to come, he would step out and find a whole new world of faith. This is something both you and I are hearing now. Jesus is saying, "It is I, now come."

The Bar District

A group of us believers had been meeting several times per week in the downtown area. We would gather together, in communion, and listen to what it was that God was saying through His Word. Funny thing is, a majority of the time we would meet in cigar lounges. Weird, I know.

Though the room was filled with smoke, which I was not particularly fond of, it was more condensed with the Spirit of God. We were available and open to anyone who would walk into the room from the outside lounge to hear hope and availability for the first time.

We were a multi-denominational church. I'm pretty sure there is none of that in this country. We didn't care about what church we attended, where our small groups met, or the diverse belief systems that have been traditionalized in religion. We just wanted to gather and become love.

There is something about the downtown area that attracts individuals. There are the lavish boutique shops, the gourmet dogs, fine dining, and nighttime entertainment. Just behind the window seal of our room, we looked upon the horizon behind us. We noticed a lively street where the bar district lit up at night.

Every week we would gather, we kept looking back to this community. Then it hit us. Where would Jesus go? Would He be comfortably sitting in church? Hanging out with other pastors? Attending a Bible study? Or maybe, just maybe, He would go hang out with drunkards in the bar district?

I have a new acronym for that now, WWJG? (Where Would Jesus Go). I'm going to make a bracelet. Maybe you'll buy it? Though I'm not very good at designing bracelets, I knew there was something about the bar district that was attracting us, not the booze by any means, but the place Jesus would have *gone*. So, we made plans for the next week to witness in the darkest alleys of the bar district. This was going to be risky. Actually, this was going to be flat out stupid.

There is something about Jesus's life that others did not agree with. He sat with sinners and tax collectors, who were some of the most unlawful people. The Pharisees would ridicule Jesus for His behavior. "And when the Pharisees saw *it,* they said to His disciples, 'Why does your teacher eat with tax collectors and sinners?'" (Matthew 9:11). Some translations actually say that the people Jesus ate with were scum.

When you take risk, it will not be acceptable among people. It will look completely different than their lifestyles. My belief is that we have been so consumed with tradition and religion on Sundays that we have become closed-minded or more like closed-churched. But Jesus came to abolish the one thing that prevented people from becoming saved. He went and sat with them in their own environment, even when it did not make sense.

The first night of the bar district was intimidating. We were surrounded by atheists, agnostics, Buddhists, and every other belief system in between. The Bible says, "But sanctify the Lord God in your hearts, and always *be* ready to *give* a defense to everyone who asks you a reason for the hope that is in you, with meekness and fear" (1 Peter 3:15). We stood on that Word as we found ourselves standing among wolves.

I want to be very clear here. We didn't come to preach to these people or to tell them to change their ways, we came as an expression of the Father's love, filtering through the crowds and having normal conversations.

Sometimes I believe we make things too complicated. For many believers it's the conversion we are after. *How many can we convert to Christianity? How many can we baptize? How many new members can we acquire?* But Paul said it very clear, "And though I have *the gift of* prophecy, and understand all the mysteries and all the knowledge, and though I have all faith, so that I could remove mountains, but have not love, I am nothing" (1 Corinthians 13:2).

No matter how much you give to the poor or how many people you convert, raise from the dead, or even baptize in a bar, if love is not your motive, you are nothing. People will not listen to what you have. You can have the most convicting signs, wave the Bible in their faces, or chant religious Scripture, but no one with listen to you. We became love by simply sitting and waiting for God's next move.

People started catching on that we were "outsiders" probably because we didn't have a drink in our hands. We were like gigantic, walking red targets with Jesus's blood on our backs. Once the seal was broken on conversations, God's Spirit began to flow.

We were asking people about their lives, their past, their failures, and their desires. We were like a Jesus vendor set up in the middle of the temple with other tax collectors, businessmen, and band members. Honestly, once we got into our element, we felt freer to open up about the reason why we were there.

Anytime you are out doing God's work, you better believe that the devil is going to attempt to throw you off track. While we were there witnessing to people, a woman had approached the group. She was a slender, blonde woman. At first, she appeared to be in our conversation, but then everything changed.

She opened up by asking us why we were there. Simply put, we told her that we were there to love people. What happened in the process was that her voice began to change. It had gone from an innocent female voice to a loud bellow. "I will annihilate you Christians!" she spoke.

Well, that just made things interesting. The group suddenly felt really uncomfortable and stepped away until it was just the woman and me. And she continued, "You think you are so cute, don't you? Out here attempting to show love. I know who Jesus is, but who are you?"

I'm pretty sure that the Jewish exorcists encountered a similar situation. They went around calling out demons from people, ". . . We exorcise you by the Jesus whom Paul preaches. . . ." And the evil spirit answered and said, 'Jesus

I know, and Paul I know; but who are you?'" (Acts 19:13–15).

This was nothing new to me as I had encountered evil spirits before. One I remember from back in the ER when an intoxicated individual came in for detox, closed me up in a room, and mimicked everything I had said to him but in a different voice just like this woman. I responded in the best way I knew how, "In the name of Jesus, spirit be gone!" And the man reverted to his original self.

The same went with this woman. In the middle of the bar district, I spoke with authority, "In the name of Jesus, spirit be gone!" And suddenly, after multiple attempts, the woman's voice came back to its original form, and she walked away as if nothing happened. Spooky!

Know this: anytime you are doing God's work in an uncertain area, be ready for the devil to pounce. He does not like active Christians messing up his plan to see others fall. You may not have ever encountered a situation like this. I will go on to say this: be bold. Do not be afraid because the Lord your God goes with you wherever you go and will never give you more than you can handle. He is looking for obedient vessels who will step foot into the darkness and bring out as many victims as possible. He was definitely using us.

We had spent weeks ministering and loving people in the bar district. There happened to be a man one evening who was resting up against the bar smoking a cigarette. He had a very distinct characteristic about himself: he was wearing crutches. I was like, *Oh yeah! Here is our chance to heal this man and see the glory of God be known among the unbelievers!* So, I high stepped it over to him like a giddy schoolgirl at a Justin Bieber concert.

"Hey, man," I said.

"How's it going?" the man replied.

"I see that you're on crutches. What if God could heal your leg?" I spoke confidently.

Suddenly, there was a man he was talking with whom got really uncomfortable. He started pacing back and forth and was like, "Oh! Be careful! These guys are attempting to heal you like 'Jesus' is supposed to." You could tell he was a nonbeliever by his mocking nature. This was the opportunity we needed to show others around us the miraculous nature of God. The man allowed us to pray for him. Guess what happened? Nothing.

God, are you kidding me right now? This was your moment! To say I wasn't frustrated would be a lie. My hope was that this man would have laid down his crutches and ran through the streets of Joplin giving glory to God for his healing. But he didn't. He was still in pain.

After our glorified attempt, the man limped off back toward the bar. I was more than disappointed. But then something happened. Before the man crutched his way back into the bar, he stopped.

"Hey," the man shouted across the way, "Thank you so much for praying for me."

We paused in confusion.

"It really meant a lot that you guys cared." Then he pointed into the bar where his friends were hanging out and continued, "*None* of those guys in there care about me." He picked up his crutches and walked into the bar but not before he showed us a grin from ear-to-ear and a courtesy wave goodbye.

You see, God did not want to heal this man. He wanted something greater—to show him love. And He would do it through obedient people who would step foot into the darkness and take risk to give others an expression of His character. It was overwhelming to see a man feel compassion for the first time. The funny thing is that he was wearing crutches because he injured his leg while being intoxicated on top of a counter and falling to the ground the night before. He was going back to the same place where he was injured, and no one cared.

We as humans are so self-destructive. What brings us turmoil and pain is more than likely the same bed we made ourselves up in. We always go back to what hurts, what doesn't make sense, and what makes us feel more lost. The good news is that Jesus came not to condemn the lost but to save them. It is the expressive characteristic of God that He would send His one and only Son into the world to *save* us from ourselves.

We attempted to save this man from going back to his old life. I believe that he was shown the love of the Father. When the timing was right, he would look back on this situation and have a revelation. It didn't matter about the conversion, the healing, or showing off. It was about a Father who desperately wants to show His compassion for others in their most self-destructive behavior. For this man, he got a wink from God and felt the love of Him through a few obedient men who would take risk and step foot into the unknown.

What about you? Have you taken risk in your life? Is fear holding you back? The unknown? Some of the most successful people in this world took a risk. For believers, risk can be replaced with faith. Have you taken your *faith* to new extremes?

This is where your burn notice can be taken to new levels, by believing God for a thought that was extreme or didn't make sense. In fact, the idea was so off the charts that you knew it had to come from God because we, as humans, can't think that stuff up.

Reaching the lost is a part of your faith. It takes risk to help those who can't help themselves. Jesus was ridiculed for helping the lost. He was put down. That didn't matter because He was about His Father's business. It didn't matter what man thought. All that mattered was what His Father thought.

Evel Knievel took risk, and it set up what would become one of the most interesting spectacles of his time. Kids wanted to be like him, and men wanted to be him. Why? Because everyone is attracted by others who take risk and become successful at it.

It doesn't take much to risk your life, but it will cost you everything. For me, it was taking risk to send out 4,000 emails and step foot into the bar district. Both situations reaped heavy rewards. I was able to reach those who were unreachable.

Ask yourself this acronym now, WWJG? Where would Jesus go? Would he go to the most extreme areas on the map? Would he sit with an addict who was needing hope? Would he visit a prisoner who had committed a heinous crime? Would he eat with tax collectors? Would he break bread with sinners? You bet. Because it's not so much what we can't do but more about what God can do *through* us. Risk is uncommon, but it is essential to your exploring a whole new world of opportunity.

Marching Orders

Risk is dangerous, but it is essential. Today I want you to think of something that takes risk. If you are getting anxious just thinking about it, good, that means you are on the right track. Be careful, the devil does not like risk. He is more pleased with those who are comfortable. You are not to be comfortable. You are meant to be on fire for God. Whatever it is, whatever your thoughts, whatever the one thing it is that God is asking you to do, do it. You will see that there is a harvest being made by those who sow into good ground. Or, I'd like to say risky ground.

CHAPTER 10:
Be a Maze Runner

'm not a movie buff, but I do like a little cinema every once in a while. My daughter, on the other hand, loves her a good dose of "Wheels on the Bus" musical while my brain goes round-and-round as I continue to watch this absurd train in all kinds of different languages. Have you ever heard "Wheels on the Bus" in French? I'm pretty sure it's not even kid-friendly, but hey, what do I know? I'm just a dad.

Cinephilia is an actual term, believe it or not, that refers to a passionate interest in films, film theory, and film criticism. Of all the things you could be addicted to, movie theaters would not be my first choice. I'm like the guy on the last row, second from the end, who can barely control his bladder from the mountain of Coca-Cola I drank. You know what I'm saying.

Recently, I had sat down to watch a peculiar film. It was a fictional film about chance and bravery. The movie starts with the main character waking up to find himself in a chamber. Don't act like you have never been caged inside a chamber before—or maybe that's just me.

As the chamber elevates to its destination, he finds himself surrounded by other peers close to his age—men who are all consumed inside this organic environment with one thing surrounding them . . . walls—four of them in a square formation as high as the eyes could see.

Most of these men had been here for as long as three years with no way out. They had built a lifestyle inside these walls, growing both vegetables and designing weapons for survival mode. They had all gotten here the same way— through the same chamber with a past that they can't recall. I can relate as I can't remember what happened fifteen minutes ago, so don't judge me.

Most of them can't remember the house they lived in, the job they had, the family they grew up with, and most importantly, they couldn't remember their names at first. Luckily, after a few short days, they would remember their names and engrave them on a wall so that they wouldn't forget them later.

Supplies showed up miraculously through the same chamber. This brought up suspicion that there was something or someone behind this crazy conspiracy. They had three rules you had to abide by: 1) Do your part. 2) Never harm another peer. 3) Never go beyond those walls.

The first thing you need to understand is much of the introduction to this movie is a lot like our story. One day we awakened up in this world and wondered where we were at and what we were doing here. There are many questions that circulate in this life. Who are we? Where are we going? What will we find?

I'm not saying you woke up in a chamber. But I am saying there was a spiritual awakening in your soul when one day you woke up realizing you were in uncharted territory, being enclosed in a world that is closed off as high as the eyes could see.

The same three rules above should apply to our lives: do your part, don't harm your neighbor, but the last rule doesn't pertain to us at all. In fact, we should do just the opposite— go beyond the walls. What's on the other side though? That's something you will have to learn for yourself.

Doing your part is a lot like running your race. Everyone has a calling in his or her life. Or, I like to call it a race. Races are not actually meant to be competitive. That's what happens in the spiritual world when everyone is competing against one another. Why? I can't quite figure that out.

Listen to what Paul says, "Do you not know that those who run in a race all run, but one receives the prize? Run in such a way that you may obtain *it*" (1 Corinthians 9:24). And he goes on, "And everyone who competes *for the prize* is temperate in all things . . ." (1 Corinthians 9:25).

The world loves to compete. "They do it to obtain a perishable crown . . ." (1 Corinthians 9:25). It's a lot of wasted time but not for you and me. When we run our race, we do it to obtain an imperishable crown—the crown we will obtain in heaven for our works here on this earth. We have to do our part—whatever that looks like to you. Will you fail? You bet. Will you win? Most certainly. But you have to run your race in such a way to obtain the prize. What prize? The prize of *certainty*.

Your life is not ordinary. In fact, God made you specifically for a purpose. Everything that is designed in this world—from the clothes we wear, to the Ninja blenders we use, to the nails holding up our pictures, to the foundation of your home—has a purpose. And let me tell you this: God's image is spread among His people so that He could bring His glory here to earth for a certain *purpose.*

If we don't do our parts, we miss the big picture. We become stagnant. We lose focus. We gravitate toward negligence. Jesus said this, "I know your works, that you are neither cold nor hot. I could wish you were cold or hot!" (Revelation 3:15). These are hard-to-swallow words, but they are spot on. If we would be on fire for the kingdom, people would see our passion and be turned by it.

Lukewarm Christianity is a scary place to be. Jesus even continued, "So then, because you are lukewarm, and neither cold nor hot, I will vomit you out of My mouth" (Revelation 3:16). All God wants is for us to do our part. It should never come out of performance but more out of position. You, in all your anointing, have the power and ability to be an inferno, burning like never before.

Never harm another neighbor is another good rule to have as well. Jesus Himself said, "You shall love your neighbor as yourself" (Mark 12:31). It is the second of the two greatest commandments Jesus gave that comes right after loving your God with all your heart, soul, mind and strength. Why not love your neighbor?

But the last rule I want you and I to focus on is never go beyond those walls. People all the time will tell you to *stay within your means, never take risk, and be cautious before you act.* Skeptics love to paralyze your dreams and prevent you from becoming a better you. Sure, people will have lots of inspirational thoughts about you but to take risk? That's unheard of.

I want to stamp this slogan above your life, "Go beyond those walls!" It's beyond the walls where you will find your burn notice, not within the walls. There are two types of faith: human faith and godly faith. The two are completely different.

Human faith involves when you and I both know that if we implement something, we can expect a certain result. For instance, I know if I go to work, I will be able to pay my bills. Obviously, I have to show up on time and do my job, but the outcome is the same—I get a paycheck. Or if I raise my children in a good environment, the likelihood of them being successful is probable. Sure, they will be defiant at times and may get into a little bit of trouble, but who didn't as a child? These are all examples of human faith. It's knowing what I can do within my own walls.

Then there is the power of godly faith. These are the individuals who step out into the unknown, who trust the invisible, and go beyond their walls. Godly faith is a difficult trust system to follow, but it is impeccable to see God's divine intervention for your life. I didn't get to where I am today by sticking with my human faith. I shattered the glass of godly faith by listening and obeying. And that, my friends, is where everything changes.

Can we trust God with our lives? Can we be obedient even when it doesn't make sense? I promise you that nothing you do for God will make sense. That's where faith comes into play. Faith is believing in something before it even happens. It's a powerful tool where you and God meet in the middle and an explosion of grace foregoes your life, ultimately leading you down a path of certainty. And there it is—the prize of certainty, knowing you and God are in this burn notice together. A partnership. Cohabiting. Living beautifully in relationship with one another.

What Thomas, the main character in the movie, figured out was that he was not in a normal vacation spot, and he most certainly wasn't dreaming. Where he happened to be was at the very core of a maze. In this maze were chosen men who would go on to carry the title "runners." These men were strikingly fast and intelligent. They studied the maze daily. By day they would enter it, and by night the maze would change. Walls would shift and new portals would open, but there was always a pattern. The runners just had to figure it out.

The maze was dangerous. New men were considered "greenies" due to their inexperience. There was no way any greenie would be able to step foot into the maze because their rules forbid it. The thing about Thomas was that he was not like the others: he was curious. He was not intimidated by the maze, and he wanted to step foot outside the walls. His curious nature from the start wanted to dissect this maze and find a way out.

What lurked on the outside of the walls was beyond them. Some people went in but never came out. Just beyond the walls was the enemy waiting for when the runners became bold, and at just the right time, they would sting them, causing them to change into something they never thought they'd be.

One day, Thomas sneaked past the authorities and entered the maze. This was against every protocol they had implemented within the system. Thomas saw the injured runner just beyond the walls and knew he was supposed to enter through the gates. And as he did the walls came closing behind him, and he found himself stuck right in the middle of the maze, which seemingly became the darkness.

Thomas was a risk taker. He didn't care about his own safety, but he was more concerned about others. Jesus was a Man concerned with others. He did not come to this earth to be served but to serve others. We can learn a lot from Thomas. He was a man on a mission stuck in the middle of a maze with no agenda, no game plan, but just faith.

Thomas now was identified as a maze runner. He was not comfortable with staying within the walls when there was a whole maze to explore, and realistically, the maze was the only way out of this uncertain abyss. This earth is a maze. It's always changing and always an adventure. That's the thing: you get one life to live this thing out, so it is up to you and me to become maze runners.

Be a maze runner in your city. What does that look like? How do I get there? Well, to be honest, it's going to take two things: getting rid of your fear and navigating yourself by faith. Fear can consume us, but faith can catapult us. It's either one or the other, but it cannot be both.

Listen to Jesus's words, ". . . For assuredly, I say to you, if you have faith as a mustard seed, you will say to this mountain, 'Move from here to there,' and it will move; and nothing will be impossible for you" (Matthew 17:20). Now, I don't know about you, but I love moving mountains. It takes what seems impossible with man, yet all is possible with God.

"For God did not give you a spirit of fear, but of power and of love and of a sound mind" (2 Timothy 1:7). Fear has no place in your heart. In fact, fear does nothing but attempt to paralyze you from your calling. You were created to multiply and bring the kingdom of God here to earth so that others may feel and know there is a God who loves them. Thomas was a man who cared for people. I mean, he would have never stepped foot inside the maze if he didn't.

What happened along the process was that Thomas was fueling others with the same passion. The tribe had become stagnant for some time. But with Thomas's inspiration they, too, believed they could do all things—together.

There is a disciple Jesus cared for who was one of the twelve disciples. His name was Thomas as well. But he carried a different name by others—doubting Thomas. Now, I don't know about you, but if I was one of the closest ones next to Jesus, my other name would have been sideswiped Aaron, but let's be honest. How many of us are a lot like the second Thomas? Doubting Thomas?

In John chapter 20, doubting Thomas was skeptical at first when he had heard that Jesus had risen from the dead. He made the not-so-popular phrase, "Unless I see in His hands the print of the nails, and put my finger into the print of the nails, and put my hand into His side, I will not believe" (John 20:25). That is a pretty heavy statement. But for many who read this sentence, it's relational. There are a lot of people out there who need to see to believe.

One week later the disciples were in the upper room, and the door was locked. Suddenly, Jesus comes spiritually through the wall and says, "Peace to you" (John 20:26). And after His first statement to the disciples, "Then he said to Thomas, 'Reach your finger here, and look at My hands; and reach your hand *here,* and put *it* into My side. Do not be unbelieving, but believing!'" (John 20:27).

Thomas went from doubting Thomas to believing Thomas in an instant. No longer was he spewing words of doubt. Instead, he was proclaiming words of hope! Hallelujah! Our King lives!

You and I can relate with doubting Thomas. Sometimes we may feel the presence of God with us, and sometimes we won't. Our walks with God are not about feelings at all, but they're about obedience and trust—two impeccable characteristics that we must have in order to become a maze runner.

Where is God calling you now? Is He asking you to step outside the walls where there is uncertainty? Does he want you to trust with complete, reckless obedience? That's where you will find His people: on the outside capturing people who are in need of a Savior and in desperate need of rescue. We are to be forerunners for the gospel, thinking of ourselves less than the least of these.

Thomas became a forerunner for the maze. He assembled clusters of armies who constantly went into the maze to study it and understand its algorithm. He understood two things: they *were* difference makers and likely the key to everything.

You must be like maze runner Thomas, not doubting Thomas. Both of them have been on the side of knowing, and both of them have been on the side of unknowing. It's a rollercoaster of emotions, this gospel, but that's the best thing about it. You have a God who fully is in control of your life. It's not yours, so therefore, it's not yours to figure out. The Bible says, "A man's heart plans his way, But the LORD determines his steps" (Proverbs 16:9).

It is a powerful tool Thomas used when strategically encrypting the maze. Over time, they were able to get out and find themselves on an adventure that would take them deeper, further, and greater than ever before. They just had to believe. This earth is your course. It is your maze. You are to be a runner for the kingdom by going out, studying it, learning it, and gathering people who are ready to tackle this thing together.

What Thomas learned out of this entire situation was that they were the key to everything. Without their skills or nature, the maze would surely win. But, ". . . He who is in you is greater than he who is in the world" (1 John 4:4). So, go out, run like never before, and become a key element to the gospel that is continuing with your life. Go be a maze runner!

Marching Orders

The world you live in now is a maze. It is faceted with changing events and uneventful outcomes. But you are not to allow fear to get the best of you, keeping you comforted inside your life. Instead, you are called to be a maze runner. One who uses faith as a guide. Find ways to step outside your comfort zone. Get involved with others who are already running. Sometimes you need a boost of passion from others to fuel your own burn notice. Remember, it's not about how you do it but rather about taking your first step toward the unknown. Run as if your life depended on it.

CHAPTER 11:

Growing Pains

We were finally home. Back at ground zero where God placed us from the very beginning at the park. I have to admit, there had been a wave of emotions during this journey. But if there are two things that I am confident of, it is that God is faithful, and His promises are everlasting.

There was something about the streets that attracted me. I'm not sure if it was the spontaneity, the irregular schedule, the sloppy joes on a Sunday afternoon sliding off the edge of the picnic tables, or the faces of those who had nothing. That was just it: if you had to picture church here at the park, it would have been symbolized by picnic tables as our pews and a pavilion as our platform. There were no walls here; therefore, there was no separation. We were completely open, and this was something that invited the crowds effortlessly.

We had done a 180-degree zero turn back to the park from multiple destinations around the city. I'm not sure if God was taking us on a wild goose chase or if He had something up His sleeve all along. But whatever the case was, it always came down to two things: loving my neighbor and equipping others to do the same.

Sometimes God will take you back to your roots to find out the authenticity of your heart. For us, ministry started getting the best of us, and, at times, we found ourselves being conformed to religious practices, doing things by getting caught in the web of routine. I think many people get caught up in doing things just because they belong to a checklist that we believe God wants us to follow. But to me, that's religion. When we start taking out the reason *why* we serve and filling it with *just because* we are supposed to serve, that's religion.

Have you ever found yourself serving just because it was routine? Everyone else is doing it, so why shouldn't I? Routines are a part of life. It's what keeps our children stationary and protects us parents from going insane. But routine, as far as walking with God, is religion. It hinders what Paul meant when he said, "And now abide faith, hope, love, these three; but the greatest of these is *love*" (1 Corinthians 13:13). We had conquered faith and love really well but seemed to place love on the back-burner. Not that we intended to fall into loveless practice, it just seemed to creep its way through the back door.

After being instructed by God to go back to the park, everything changed. It was kind of like going back to the basics. For me, it was the foundation where I was moved to love people unconditionally. And for others, it was a passion that persuaded others to do the same.

We had been faithfully serving the streets back at the park once again. Months had passed, and the flood gates of God's blessings came pouring in. Little did I know there was more to this story. God was about to swing us in a direction that no one saw coming. He was about to open a door that wouldn't just be a small crack in the ground. He was about to open the floodgate of immeasurable breakthrough.

Washington Hope Center

I happened to be at work one day when I received a peculiar phone call.

"Yes, is this Aaron with S.O.S. Ministries?" the voice spoke through the phone.

"Yes, this is he," I responded.

"I heard that you were looking for a building?" He continued.

Now, I didn't know if this guy was messing with me or if someone was playing a dirty trick, but I do not recall ever looking for a building. The man on the phone happened to be one of the superintendents of the Joplin School District. He continued to tell me about a school that was located on the east side of Joplin next to a baseball stadium. The one that was revealed to us at the Broadway Bash.

"Aaron, we have a school called Washington Education Center that is up for sale, and we want you to place a bid on the building."

Being the calculator behind every decision I make, I was like, *Uh, dude, we don't have any money or resources to take on an entire school. So, I don't know what you want us to bid on this building?* Little did I know those words came out of my mouth.

"Well, we can't technically by law give it to you for free, but we can give it to you for one dollar," the superintendent responded.

I paused through the phone before I said anything out of line. *One-stinking-dollar?* I thought to myself. This was flat crazy. Either I was going to make a decision, by faith, to place a bid for one dollar on a 20,000-square-foot, abandoned building, or I would come to the conclusion that someone else needed this more than we did. So, as a group, we made the ridiculous decision to place a bid on the school for, you guessed it, one-messily-dollar. Any bid above ours would take ownership easily before us.

I had entered the school district with a money order for one dollar. The check itself probably cost more than one dollar to print—even the bank was thrown off by my amount to a school district. I'm pretty sure they called the IRS to red flag my withdrawal, but hey, a dollar saved is a dollar earned, right?

I had made the decision to write a professional letter and place it inside the envelope, explaining what we would do with the building. After much consideration, we thought that what this building needed was a makeover, not necessarily to renovate what appeared to be broken but to reinvent people's lives by opening up the facility as a community center. This repurposing would give people both hope and encouragement along the way.

I had inserted both the letter and the one-dollar money order and dropped it off at the front desk.

Months went by, and we heard nothing. Actually, we had forgotten about the building altogether because we knew it would be a long shot if we did obtain the school. Without an agenda, we continued to serve the streets and love people.

I had been sitting in the living room, playing with my daughter when I received a phone call. It was actually a text. My buddy from the school board had messaged me.

"Congrats on your new purchase!" Jeff texted me through my phone.

Purchase? I had to think quickly. *New vehicle? Something for my daughter? Our house we just purchased months ago?* I was completely blank with what his text should have meant to me. Then suddenly, it hit me like a pile of bricks. *The school!*

Then I was responding back to him faster than my thumbs could type. "You're talking about the school, right?" I texted.

"Yes, silly! You guys have won the bid for Washington Education Center!" Jeff responded.

I'm not sure what a stroke feels like, but I'm pretty sure my legs gave out underneath me. I could barely get back up before I ran into the kitchen shouting words of victory. Or maybe my speech came out garbled toward my wife.

"Babe! We have won the bid for the school!" I shouted.

"Congrats!" she shouted back.

Like two varsity football players, my wife and I had done a victorious chest bump in mid-air. Things were going to move fast as Jeff wanted us and the team to come to the school board meeting that night to claim our prize. There was little time to gather some of the team members as we made our way into the school board meeting. We were moving so fast that I can't recall if I even put underwear on before we left the house. Ah, who cares!

We entered the school and opened the double doors to the meeting where we were standing in the middle of a surge of media and board members. The news station was shooting video, and the board members had asked me to come to the front. I didn't even have a speech thought out!

The school board members and the people all congratulated us on our endeavor. I thanked all of them for their choice, and they were excited about the facility continuing to be used for the sake of the community. We overheard there was another bidder. A developer who wanted to demolish the school and build apartments, but at the last minute, surprisingly, they opted out of their bid, and with the letter I wrote about the building being a community center, they knew it was the perfect fit—like "a marriage" the school board announced. Coincidence or something more?

You see, God honors those who are obedient to His divine purpose. We had spent years out in the streets serving and feeding the "least of these." We were a church without walls, and now God was going to give us a school with walls, not just for us but also for the people around us. Growth does not necessarily come from spending years inside a church with much, but rather growth comes from those who are faithful with little. Before long God will give you much—20,000 square feet of much!

The school was called Washington Education Center, and it had been a school for elementary kids through generations of students. We had started meeting the neighbors, and many of them had gone to school here and were excited about the transformation happening. The team and I had strategically thought of what we would call our new home. And after much consideration it came clearly. We wanted to preserve the history of the building so Washington was a good title. What would we call the last part? Well, we knew that what we had developed was hope. Lots of it. So, it was a no-brainer. Washington Hope Center is what we would call it.

S.O.S. Ministries and Washington Hope Center were a good fit. We soon identified ourselves with the tagline, "A cry for help. A place of hope." because that is exactly who we were. Like Morse code, people had been tapping tones where we would hear their cries and meet them where they were at—much like the coast guard.

Jesus was a Man after people's cries. God the Father had heard His children's cries and sent His Son to help those who were in need, ultimately providing hope to the hopeless. We could relate a lot with Jesus. We had stepped outside the four walls and became available to those who were without, overlooked, and misused. Who knew we would go on to obtain an entire school for one dollar!

God's plans for your life are infinite. In fact, they are everlasting. Each day you wake up is another opportunity to live, learn, and grow into the individual He created you to be. But much of what God blesses you with is not necessarily used for your consumption. Sometimes you will have to make drastic decisions—painful decisions.

The building needed some work. Evidently, the school was structurally sound. There were some leaks through the roof, paint had been peeling from the walls, some doors would open, and some wouldn't, but ultimately the building was standing.

After many months of waiting for money to open the doors, God spoke to me, "Why aren't you using the facility I gave to you?" This was a heart check. *He's right, why don't we open the doors to feed the people?* And what better way to open up the facility than to paint and prep the center room to start feeding the people around the neighborhood?

We took cubicle carpet from other rooms and placed them in the auditorium. That would cover the retched floor. The walls were painted with a color I would call prison grey. Not very inviting to say the least, so we repainted them with neutral colors. The place was being transformed into an auditorium of reinvention. Not just restoring what was old and making it new again, but we were taking old lives and reinventing them to become something spectacular.

God loves to take what was once old and make it new again. For many, this school was abandoned and useless, but to God it was meant to be filled and given new purpose. And He would use a bunch of unqualified servants to open up the doors and invite them into God's new, restored, reinvention center.

The next Sunday we would open the doors to Washington Hope Center. Luckily, we were able to get the bathrooms working and the alarm system activated. Many people from the park came to be a part of history but so did many from the neighborhood. Same agenda: be available and love unconditionally.

We had the privilege of meeting many people from the community. Some were poor, some broken, others addicted, and many were looking for hope. We were able to pray and see God miraculously transform lives. We saw addictions cease, broken relationships restored, jobs obtained, and children reconciled back to their parents. There was endless opportunity here at Washington Hope Center. After all, we lived by the slogan, "A cry for help. A place of hope."

But after months of serving the people at the Hope Center, money was drying up. We couldn't get sponsors to help us bring this place to life. We started having break-ins. The roof was leaking bad and would cost too much for us to fix. I'll be honest, I was stressing about the building and found myself, well, becoming hopeless.

Then, one day, God gave me a word, "Partnership." I knew one of the known homeless shelters in the area was looking for a family shelter, and I thought this place would be a perfect fit to shelter women and children who were going through temporary homelessness.

I had established a great relationship with the founder of the shelter. He and I had a lot in common as far as seeing the church thrive and helping those who were in need. So, I had invited him over to the school to see how we could partner.

I had given them a tour of the facility, showing them the potential. We had sat down to discuss what this place would look like and how they could be a part of the big picture. He loved it. Everything about it. Unfortunately, all he saw was money. It would cost too much for him and his staff to come in and open a homeless shelter if he didn't take *ownership* of the building. This did not settle well in my stomach. It had hit me like a sledgehammer to the chest.

Have you ever been to a point in your life where God had given you something only to go on to feel disappointment all at the same time? For me, this building had taken years to obtain. Countless hours. Countless Sundays. Countless obedience. And now I came to a point where I had to decide if would I continue to gain support for the building or hand it over to another organization? Needless to say, my discomfort reached new heights.

Following God takes obedience. It takes sacrifice. You can't grow with God unless you go through seasons of pain where much of what is going on does not make sense. If it did, you would be the one in charge and not Him. The question really is: are we building our *own* kingdom or are we building *His* kingdom?

Many of us want to control the situation. Sure, we want to use God's name at the top, but ultimately are we willing to give up the one thing God has given us so that His church can continue to grow? That's growing pains. It hurts. It will stretch you. But God is looking for your obedience over your sacrifice. Let me let you in on a little secret, "To obey is better than sacrifice. . . ." (1 Samuel 15:22).

We had sacrificed a lot of our time. We had been obedient with what God had given to us. At times, I wondered which one we were doing more—sacrificing to obtain or being obedient to the point of discomfort. That's a good point here: unless we are being obedient to the point of discomfort, there is a good chance we are not being obedient all. For me, this was beyond discomforting: this was torture.

I knew of nowhere else to go but to the prayer room, asking many times where to go from here. God had given us such a blessing: I knew that it was meant to be. But what do you do with a building God has given to you? Do you continue to press in? Do you attempt to labor in vain? After much prayer and observation, it just made sense to hand it over to the organization. Every need would be filled since they had credibility in the community and funds to bring this place to life.

So, we made the decision to hand over the building to the homeless shelter, and they would transform the school into a family shelter for women and children. How awesome! What's crazy about the process is that we had received donations specifically for women and children. It was as if God was setting up what He already intended to happen. That's the thing: God will never revert on His promises.

The school district would have never given the school to a homeless shelter. They would, however, give it to an organization who wanted to convert it into a community center. And this center would eventually open the doors to another organization with the same mindset, who would transform this school into a family shelter, giving both women and children an opportunity to receive—you guessed it—hope.

Win One

Jesus was a man who was always after the one. In fact, He would do everything in His power to leave everyone for that one lost sheep. Matthew chapter 18 gives the illustration, "What do you think? If a man has a hundred sheep, and one goes astray, does he not leave the ninety-nine and go to the mountains to seek that one that is straying?" (Matthew 18:12).

To be honest, we as the church often love numbers. We believe success is found in the amount of people we see each Sunday. If the Sunday attendance is scarce, then we often ask ourselves what we did wrong the week prior. Jesus, however, was not about the numbers, but He was about the *one*.

Sometimes in order to grow we have to think small. What can happen along our journey through life is that we can negate the one individual who needs God by being consumed with the crowd. Crowds are an attractive place to find ourselves (unless you have agoraphobia), but we can miss the opportunity of finding others who are in desperate need of attention.

What I have learned along the way is that most of my encounters have come through individuality. Spending one-on-one time with others who are in need. I have witnessed widows downpouring their tears on the pavement, I have seen tumors shrink inside the brain of one man, and I have lent my ear to others who just needed a listener. It's amazing when you grow through one another, not in crowds but in simple conversation.

"For where two or three are gathered together in My name, I am there in the midst of them" (Matthew 18:20). Why do you think the Bible only uses simple math here? Because there is power in smaller numbers. It's always the one who Jesus wants.

Think of Jesus's ministry for three and a half years on this earth. How many people did He choose? Twelve. Just twelve because He knew in order to grow you had to spend countless hours with those who would eventually grow the church. And these twelve men would go on to bring the gospel to a third of the world's population now. It's about growing in small numbers.

Speaking of numbers, I had the opportunity to be invited to a Stronger Men's Conference. This colosseum was a place full of testosterone and faith. There were over 5,000 men at this conference that was filled with keynote speakers, insurmountable worship, and yes, motocross!

On the last day of the men's conference, I had driven to the colosseum separately. I had stopped behind an SUV at a stop light. While I was glaring down at my dash, I looked up only to focus on the license plate of the vehicle in front of me. The license plate said, "Win-One." Then it dawned on me.

What if we were a generation that each won one person to Christ? What if we could win one individual every day through love and opportunity only to see their lives changed? That's burn notice. It's like a wildfire. We live in a world of dryness. If we would set a fire in one individual, that individual would go on to ignite fires in others, ultimately, causing a wildfire of God's presence. But how did that wildfire start? Through winning one!

This license plate would ignite a whole new world of understanding. We get so fixed on the numbers that we lose focus on the one. Jesus did not lose focus of the one. He said, "And if he should find it, assuredly, I say to you, he rejoices more over that sheep than over the ninety-nine that did not go astray" (Matthew 18:13). That's unheard of! If I had any shepherd instinct, I would collect the sheep I had and forget my loss, but that is not the case with Jesus. He would leave everyone else just to gather His lost sheep. "Even so it is not the will of your Father who is in heaven that one of these little ones should perish" (Matthew 18:14).

If we want to grow in the kingdom of God, we are going to have to let go of some things we have held on to. Obedience is greater than sacrifice. What are some things you could be obedient in today? Are they discomforting?

Do they stretch you? Maybe God has been telling you to let some things go because He has a greater purpose for you. When we sacrifice what God has sustained, He will take us to a whole new level. Likewise, if we want to grow, we are going to have to simplify our lives, not minimizing our possessions but minimizing our mindset by going after the one lost sheep. Numbers are great, but heaven rejoices over the one lost sheep because everyone is important to God. You're important. I'm important. Not one goes unaccounted for.

Pumping gas is something you and I do religiously. Luckily for me, I bought a fuel-efficient vehicle. One day I had stopped at the gas station only to find out the store had closed down, so I took my happy self down to the next convenient store. Once I had stepped out of the vehicle, I noticed the card reader was out of order. Great.

I had walked myself into the gas station where I approached the teller whose name was Destiny. Weird. After exiting the building, pushing off my already frustrated emotions, I was approached by an African American woman.

"Sir, could you spare some change for gas?" The woman spoke.

"Sure, I'll help you out," I replied.

As we were walking back to our cars, I wanted to get to know this needy woman. I asked her where she was from. She told me she grew up in this town but was on her way up north to stay with a friend. Eager to know her situation because I'm just nosy like that, she told me she just left a halfway house for relapsing on drugs.

I then knew it was time to open up about my life as well. Coincidently, she was moved by my story and began to open up, too. I shared the gospel with her and the distance God had taken me. She then told me that she used to be a pastor's daughter but got caught up in homosexuality and was kicked out of the church. Shortly after, she became a drug addict and felt lost in her ways.

I sat there and listened. Not once did I judge her for her decisions, but instead I saw her for who she was—a child of God, the one lost sheep. And then I lifted her up with my words. She was so moved by the presence of God that I had to ask her, "Have you ever given your life to Christ?" Oddly enough, she told me that she never had given her life to Christ, and she was a pastor's daughter.

But on this day, she vocalized her life to Christ. She was ready to receive Him. Not by what I said to her but by the Shepherd who came to find the one lost sheep. So right there in the middle of all the chaos, at the center of a gas station, next to her vehicle, surrounded by a crowd of witnesses, she gave her life to Christ. Needless to say, heaven started shouting from the rooftop as this woman would go on to surrender her life and be made new all because I wasn't focused on the numbers but—more than anything—after winning the one.

Marching Orders

Growing is painful. As we mature in God's kingdom, we will be asked to do some pretty out-of-the-normal things. Don't be timid because of this but instead be obedient.

You may have sacrificed a lot, but when it comes time to implement, think of how you can increase the kingdom through one act of obedience. If you want to grow, you will have to think small. Stop focusing on numbers as a sign of growth and begin winning one at a time. There were twelve dedicated disciples who would expand the church, and there will be individuals, like you and I, who are dedicated to simplifying their lives through one act of obedience after another. What is God asking you to be obedient with today? It may be your one obedient move that creates a wave of opportunity. Go now and multiply through smaller numbers!

CHAPTER 12:

Sold Out

I f you are like 59 percent of Americans, there is a good chance that you have been a sports fan at some point or another. On average, in football alone, nearly 18.6 million people find themselves giddy over a little pig skin. I'm from Missouri, which means unless you bleed Kansas City Chief red, then you're an outsider. Seriously, try wearing black and grey in this neck of the woods, and you will more than likely find yourself running for your life. I've seen it, and it's not pretty.

I had the privilege of attending a Kansas City Chiefs' game where we hit a record as the loudest stadium in history at 142.2 decibels worth of noise. If you want to get technical, a jet take-off is about 150 decibels, and a thunderclap ranked in at 120 decibels.[13]

We pretty much stood between the sound of a jet and a thunderclap. If that wasn't enough, the announcer wanted us to get louder. Seriously though, the volume of voices that surrounded me along with the feet banging the stadium floor was enough to throw me into a seizure. Luckily, I don't have a history of epilepsy.

Decked out in all red with Chiefs' emblems underneath our eyes and a jaw-dropping shout, you could tell we were a part of the fan base. That day Kansas City made history. With the *Guinness World Book of Records* present on the field with their decibel meter, everyone anticipated the record to be a part of Chiefs' kingdom, and obtaining it we did.

Sports are ridiculously addictive. They are a great way to bring people together, wear some silly paint over their faces, and dive nose deep into a character they never knew existed—*fandomania*! Ruled by competition and camaraderie, it's safe to say there is no lack of demand when it comes to the sports world.

On this day, the entire stadium was sold out. There was a mixture of kids, adolescents, adults, and yes, even an eighty-one-year-old grandpa who was shirtless! But everyone was on the same page, trying to make history while supporting one of the best teams we thought had a chance at a title.

Though I was overwhelmed by the nature of the people here and was moved by their sportsmanship, I couldn't help but notice there was a difference between being a fan and being on the team. Being in the stands was great, but what if you were on the sidelines with some of the greatest athletes? That would be something special.

Spectator or Servant

There is a huge difference between being a fan and being a follower. As a sports fan I am really good at understanding the statistics and names of the players—even the record of the team and their schedule for the year. But I don't know what it's like to be "in the game." I simply am just a spectator in the crowd.

Jesus said some profound words that many of us will never forget, ". . . If anyone desires to come after Me, let him deny himself, and take up his cross, and follow Me" (Matthew 16:24). Jesus knew what it took to follow Him. Why? Because He wanted followers, not fans.

There are many people in the church today who are really good at attendance, showing up to a Bible study, and placing a good amount of their income in the offering basket. But, like many, if there are not the first steps toward following Jesus by denying self and picking up our cross, then we simply become fans.

Fans know statistics about Jesus, but they do not know what it's like to *be* with Jesus. Fans are really good about observing what others are doing but are not involved in what others are accomplishing. Fans know the next move, but they cease to act out, by faith, the path Jesus wants them to take. Fans can cheer, they can celebrate, they can attend, but there's one thing they lack—obedience.

Unfortunately, for many, we are okay with just sitting back and spectating. But Christ is looking for those who will serve. Kyle Idleman in his book, *Not a Fan*, stated this quote, "He is looking for more than words of belief; He's looking to see how those words are lived out in your life. When we decide to believe in Jesus without making a commitment to follow Him, we become nothing more than fans."[2]

Do you feel like you are looking from the outside in? Are you finding yourself spectating more than surrendering? God wants nothing more than complete surrender. It's laying down your life so that you can have life, giving up the one thing you were never in control of from the beginning—your life.

People in the Bible made lots of excuses why not to follow Jesus: burying their families, tending to their purchased land, the list goes on. But Jesus wasn't concerned about their excuses, He was moved by their faith. All the more, He wanted them to be servants for the kingdom, not just spectators.

As I found myself sitting in the stands, I knew there would be more fulfillment if I were with the team. Spectators don't get a taste of what the trophy feels like: they just get to observe it. But what if God was calling us to step out of the stands and onto the field? How much greater would your calling be if you locked arms with other athletes in the game? And by athletes, I mean believers who are already in the game.

I will go on to say this: get up out of the stands and start marching onto the field. You will never know what victory tastes like from afar. The kingdom of God is not about observation, for the kingdom of God lives within you. And through servanthood we see many people throughout the Scriptures who went on to do spectacular things.

David got into the game by throwing a stone at Goliath's face, winning an army who would someday follow him. Noah got in the game when he took two 4 x 4's and struck the first nail, saving the ordained people of God and starting a new world. The disciples got in the game when they dropped their fishing rods and followed the Son of God, ultimately beginning the church on what it is today. None of which they did by sitting back and observing what it would be like to follow God. Don't worry about what it *could be* when you can live by how it *should be*. By faith, these men instinctively marched down the stairs, jumped the wall, and got into the game. They went from spectator to servant. And let me tell you, everything changed when they did.

United at the Stadium

The day finally came. I found myself sitting in front of the title company, wondering if I had made the best decision of my life or if it was a desperate response to my failures. Washington Hope Center was about to have a new owner, and I couldn't help but ponder on all the hard work we had done over the past three years—three years of faith, three years of obedience, three years of failures, and everything in between. But here I was sitting at the table with a fine-tip ink pen about to sign over ownership.

I might as well have been signing over my birthright. We had only owned the building for approximately six months, which did not give us a lot of time to see it develop. Though I had been having feelings of uncertainty, I had greater emotions of peace. It sounds funny, but I knew what I was doing was right and pertained to a whole lot of obedience.

Even for you, I bet there has been inexpressible times of emotions where you did not know if you had made the right decision or not. We humans are really good at relying on our emotions. God did not ask for our feelings, but He asked for our *faith*. And to me, this was the right decision and the only way to see God's kingdom come.

We had shaken hands as the deed and title were exchanged to a new owner. We had smiled and laughed. I'm pretty sure I was tearful, but both of us had one thing on our minds—creating opportunity to open Washington Hope Center into a family shelter for women and children who had been temporarily homeless. To me, that was hope.

What's even more crazy about this adventure is that prior to me signing over the title to a new owner we had received toys for the nursery, a library full of children's books, and hygiene products for families. It's as if God was setting up the facility for just that, a family shelter. Weird, I know.

As I had exited the title company and had gotten into my car, I got a phone call. Suicide had been running rampant in our community. Just in our area alone, over seven students had committed suicide within the school year. In Missouri, suicide had increased 30 percent, so the community knew it was time to intervene. And little did I know, God was about to use me as a vessel to help prevent suicide in our area.

There was a youth rally happening at a complex in the Joplin area. I was asked to be one of the keynote speakers for the event. Without any hesitancy, I gladly accepted the opportunity. Prior to the event, a group of us leaders in the community decided to have a prayer meeting. Sure, we could have events that raise awareness, but what was it that God wanted to do for this city? The answer would come in a vision.

As the circle of men started praying, I stopped and asked God for His heart. You will find throughout your walk with God that, if you ask Him the right questions, He will give you the right response. *God, I know you want to change this community because there is so much brokenness, but God, what is your heart?*

And this is what I saw: My eyes were closed as I saw what appeared to be a football field in the distance. As the field got closer and closer, I found it to be empty. It was detailed to the point where I could actually see the blades of grass and the spray paint that made up the yard lines. But it was empty. Then, in an instant, people from all walks of life started stepping onto the field. These were men, women, and children, and they were all holding candle lights. It was a broad view of what symbolized the community. The candles signified hope. And as the vision continued, the people started coming together, closer and closer, until there was perfect unity. I was actually telling the others about my vision as I saw it come into focus, and then it was over.

"Aaron, that's it!" the men responded.

"What's it?" I questioned back.

"We need to have a night of unity at a stadium!"

I had found myself in a different predicament than ever before. What God had spoken to me before was through His voice, and now He was giving me instructions through His *visions*.

So, I started making phone calls. I spoke with friends of mine on the school board who would bring this idea to the school administration. And next thing I knew was that the Joplin School District would allow us to have an event, which we eventually called United at the Stadium, at Junge Field!

I want you to understand the magnitude here. We had gone from serving the streets for years, loving and feeding people, which would ultimately create opportunity to obtain an entire school for one dollar, and after obediently signing the Hope Center to a new owner, the moment I got into my vehicle, God laid suicide on my heart to which now He has me in a different season where we would fill stadiums. So, you see, I was handing over a Hope Center because God had different plans for my life.

The same goes for you. God's promises are everlasting, and they never change. What you have sacrificed, God will fill. What you have let go of, God will exchange for something greater. What you have lost, God will bring new life to what was once dead. It's the grace of God. It's because of His character that you and I have the opportunity to go deeper, higher, and further than ever before. "Now to Him who is able to do exceedingly abundantly above all that we ask or think, according to the power that works in us" (Ephesians 3:20).

Well, I had found myself in an immeasurable moment where I knew there was a new season for my life, and it would be my goal to prevent teen suicide from happening in our community. That is my life: to create hope in broken situations.

Next thing I knew, businesses, organizations, and churches started calling me after they had heard about United at the Stadium. This was nothing new to me because I knew God's character. Just like the Broadway Bash, where finances and people started pouring in, the same was happening for United at the Stadium. It's obedience first, and then comes opportunity.

Before I knew it, we were fully funded in less than one month. The community started hearing about this event and struck a match. Parents, coaches, and students became encouraged by this movement and knew it was something the community needed. Flyers were handed out, a Facebook page was made, and thousands of people came together as a body of people who would step out against the darkness.

While we were out promoting the event downtown, a fifteen-year-old boy approached our booth and was encouraged by the event. As we were concluding our conversation, he stopped me and said, "I was actually going to kill myself tonight."

I stopped everything I was doing and called the boy over to me. "Listen, I see you for who you are. That you are a child of God, and He loves you very much. Your life is important. You have purpose. Let me pray for you." As we came together in agreement, I prayed for the boy, and he felt peace for the first time. "Thank you so much for those kind words. I now know that I have purpose," said the boy as he walked away.

You see, it doesn't take much to find people who are hurting. All you have to do is be available. Whatever God has placed in your heart is meant to reach others who are broken. For me, all I was doing was promoting an event God told me to start. And low and behold, a fifteen-year-old boy would approach my booth, get rocked by the Holy Spirit, and leave fulfilled. Another life would be saved.

The event really started getting some hype. We had other nonprofits and organizations who wanted to be a part of this and help to spread the word on suicide prevention and awareness. We had developed bracelets for the event. These hope bracelets were yellow with the event, date, and a national text help hotline for anyone who was struggling. The bracelets were so popular that we handed out thousands. And when the love of God reaches a community, He would be able to find children who were in need of some hope.

Testimonies started coming in. We heard word that a middle school girl, who was found to have cuts down both of her arms, was handed a bracelet by a fellow student, where she would go on to call the hotline and get help. Grace is extending out our arms to others who we physically can tell are in need, ultimately giving them hope for the first time. Who knows how long this girl had been struggling with self-identity, but what one boy would do by just extending out his arm and handing a girl a bracelet would be the fuel she would need to change her life?

United at the Stadium went on to receive a proclamation from the mayor of the city, whereas August 15 would be known as "United at the Stadium Day" in Joplin, Missouri. The *Joplin Globe* made it a front-page story, and multiple editors from the newspaper wrote a specific story about how grand the event was and how much it impacted the community. You never know how far God wants to throw you. But be ready. When He gives you instructions on what to do next, it will never be ordinary. Your burn notice will look extraordinary! It will be a flame that, when it gets onto others, spreads like wildfire, putting passion in others' hearts who are moved by what they see people doing for God.

The thing is, God's divine purpose for you never stops. Whatever you have done in His name brings fruit to your life. It creates a wave of movement that can only bring glory to God for the works that you do. For me, it was being faithful with little to where God had given me much and still does to this day.

Coincidence or God?

I hope that you have been encouraged along this journey. Much of what I have experienced throughout my walk with God has been shown to you through this book. But there are so many more testimonies I have witnessed that could not fit in this book and still to this day are happening in my life. I wake up every day knowing there's always more. That's the formula to finding the meaning to your life: waking up every day expecting something to happen while seeking Him.

There's just one more story I want to tell you about. It's more than likely my favorite. It's a story of redemption and hope.

There was a boy I knew who grew up in a good home. He was surrounded by parents who wanted the best for his life. Growing up, his family went to a Methodist church. This was not a megachurch, but it was a rustic church comprised of close family members. The boy would attend church because his mother wanted him to, but he found himself in the back doodling on paper as the service went on.

The boy was never a bad kid. He made A's and B's and regularly attended classes. He played sports and was a part of the Boy Scouts. He liked drawing, hanging out with close friends, and spending time with family.

At age sixteen, his parents purchased his first vehicle. It was a 1990 cherry red Toyota Tercel. It might as well have been a Prius. The boy worked at a sandwich shop where he would develop his work ethic with the aroma of the homemade bread.

Over time though, something would change, and he started wanting to become popular and recognized. This would only bring bad people into his life as others wanted what he had: freedom. He would routinely pick up friends and hang out on the weekends. Eventually, one night would change everything as he stayed out late and would try meth for the first time.

Weekends would come, and he and his friends would venture out on drug binds where they would experiment with different drugs. The boy ended up becoming defiant. He would run away at age sixteen, write on a school desk that he was going to blow up the school, and fall deeper and darker into a pit of hopelessness.

His relationship with his parents became nonexistent as he isolated himself from his close relatives. After high school he met a boy who would eventually invite him over to a house to hangout. The boy showed up as he walked down the stairs of this house where the carpet was red and the furniture was black. Little did the boy know he had stepped foot into a drug house, full of meth.

The boy had once again found himself stuck in addiction and would move into the drug house. Over time, the boy became one of the biggest drug dealers in the city. He was a professional at destroying lives. He would give drugs to single mothers and parents who spent all their money and left their children abandoned. He had no compassion for others, was prideful, was a thief, and never looked out for anyone but himself.

Along the way the boy became paranoid and started seeing things that were very dark. He had made multiple attempts to admit himself to a psych ward but was always pulled back by other drug dealers. Eventually, men were out to get him because he owed so much money from his addiction.

The boy had found himself at rock bottom with nothing to show for his life but a trash bag. He had no money, no friends, no relationship with his parents, and certainly no way out. He found himself in complete desperation for change.

One night, when the drug house was empty, he knew there was no other choice but to pray. "God, if you are real, I don't want this life anymore. I need you to come into my life and change it forever." As the prayer came out, he found himself soaking the carpet with his tears and was in a position where he collapsed to his knees.

The boy didn't know what happened next, but for three days he didn't remember anything. He doesn't know if he was getting high, selling drugs, or getting beat up. Then, out of nowhere the man who invited him to live at the house was pointing his finger in his face.

"Get out of here! You don't belong here!" the man shouted.

The boy was devastated. He had nothing to show for his life, and now he was getting kicked out of the drug house with nowhere to go. The boy got into his vehicle completely emotionally wrecked, and he felt a stirring in his heart that he was supposed to go home where he would find safety.

The boy showed up at his parent's house where they didn't even recognize him. He had lost so much weight, had sores on his face, and hadn't slept in over a week. He looked like a walking corpse.

The mother, overwhelmed by the appearance of her son, told him that he could not stay there. While the boy was nearly on the brink of death, the dad encouraged the mother to let their son stay there as he could see the boy was in bad shape.

"Fine, but only if he gets clean," the mother responded.

Even though it would be the hardest decision the boy had ever made to leave his old life for a new one, that night he agreed to get clean. For the next three days he went through extreme withdrawals. But he stuck it out and continued to stay clean.

After the third day, the boy finally started feeling better, and he looked at his phone. His phone was full of text messages and voicemails of people who wanted him to come back to his old life. And in a moment, the boy would shatter his phone as it would become the turning point for his new life.

The boy stayed clean. He ended up going to college and became a registered nurse. He went on to save lives rather than destroying them. Eventually, he would go back to school and get his master's degree and become a board-certified nurse practitioner. Such transformation!

This is such a good story of redemption, faith, and hope. It is a story of the prodigal son, where God had compassion for His son who went on to live a life apart from His Father and yet, one day would return home. Do you know why this story speaks so much to me? It's because that boy was *me*. I was the lost boy who fell into drug addiction, who destroyed others' lives, and who lived a life for myself.

But now I am transformed. *Sold out*. I owe my life to God for the miraculous saving grace that granted me access into the kingdom of God. And now, what saved me gives me compassion for others who are in need of a Savior—the One who calms the wind and the storm, the One who is the Author and Finisher of my life, and the One whom I choose to follow.

Just think, for three days I didn't know what I was doing after I called out to God. But after three days I was miraculously kicked out of the drug house. It was my *resurrection*. After the Spirit of God filled my life, I was resurrected to a new life. One that I am living today.

Your life is not a coincidence. It's ordained by God. He molded you and formed you even while you were in the womb. Sure, we may have drifted off the right path, but God seeks us in our lostness. He is the One who searches our hearts and gives life to that which is dead.

I was dead—a drug dealer who was in the business of killing people spiritually. But now I have gone on from being a drug dealer to becoming a hope dealer! My life is not mine, but it's *His*.

This book was given to me three years ago, but it wasn't ready. God knew I had to be tested through the trials of life and be a testimony for others to see. You can't preach the gospel unless you have *lived* the gospel. That's what Jesus meant when He said we would be His witnesses. Today I am over sixteen years clean. Never once did I look back. I now pull others from the darkness and give them new meaning.

The same goes for your life. Burn like never before. When should you burn? The time is now. Jesus said, "The time is fulfilled, and the kingdom of God is at hand. Repent, and believe in the gospel" (Mark 1:15). We should never wait for something to happen, but we should go after our burn notice as if tomorrow was never promised. How do you keep the burn? By faith. Every day wake up expecting something to happen and then apply the Word of God to your life. It doesn't take much, but it will be palpable. You can see the character of God as you step out in faith.

Finally, burn with others! Find your fit. Get with others who are on fire for the gospel. You will see that when you lock arms with others, there is encouragement, energy, and fuel. We were never meant to walk this earth alone, but you need to burn with others who are passionate for the kingdom of God.

"And whatever you do, do it heartily, as to the Lord and not to men, knowing that from the Lord you will receive the reward of the inheritance; for you serve the Lord Christ" (Colossians 3:23). Bring heaven here to earth through your life, begin a movement, love without any agenda, sow seed, transform, utilize the Holy Spirit, create opportunity, take risk, be a maze runner, grow every day, and above all, be sold out to the gospel.

"For our God is a consuming fire" (Hebrews 12:29). And because He is a consuming fire, we have the ability to express who He is. When you find your burn notice, be prepared because God will take you places you have never been and areas of the earth you have never experienced.

"But as it is written: 'Eye has not seen, nor ear heard, Nor have entered into the heart of man The things which

God has prepared for those who love Him" (1 Corinthians 2:9). Go now and multiply.

About the Author

A. M. Garcia is a visionary, influential speaker, and best-selling author of *Coincidence or God?* He is the Founder of S.O.S. Ministries, Inc. a nonprofit that works toward bettering the community and reaching the lost in the streets. Aaron is known for creating movements such as The  Broadway Bash, Washington Family Hope Center, and United at the Stadium. He holds his master of science in nursing and is a board-certified nurse practitioner. Aaron, his wife, and three children all reside in Neosho, Missouri

You can follow A. M. Garcia @:
Website:
www.authoramgarcia.com

Facebook:
www.facebook.com/authoraaron
Twitter:
www.twitter.com/AaronMGarcia1

LinkedIn:
www.linkedin.com/in/a-m-garcia-4017aab8/

ENDNOTES

Chapter 3: Love without Agenda

1. Gary D. Chapman, *The 5 Love Languages: The Secret to Love That Lasts* (Chicago: Northfield Publishing, 2015) 38.

2. "Love." Merriam-Webster. Accessed November 15, 2018. https://www.merriam-webster.com/dictionary/love.

3. Marisa Donnelly, "36 Definitions of Love, According to Urban Dictionary." Thought Catalog. September 28, 2017. Accessed November 15, 2018. https://thoughtcatalog.com/marisa-donnelly/2016/04/36-definitions-of-love-according-to-urban-dictionary/.

Chapter 5: Transformation>Change

1. P. T. Barnum, *Struggles and Triumphs: Or, Forty Years Recollections of P. T. Barnum* (London: Forgotten Books, 2017), 621–637.

2. James Strong, *The New Strongs Expanded Exhaustive Concordance of the Bible* (Nashville: Thomas Nelson, 2010), 162.

3. Ibid, 20.

4. Ibid, 162.

5. Ibid, 162.

Chapter 9: Risk Takers

1. "Legendary Evel," Evel Knievel, Accessed November 18, 2018, http://evelknievel.com/the-man/.

2. Ibid.

3. "Most Broken Bones in a Lifetime, *Guinness World Records*, Accessed November 18, 2018, http://www.guinnessworldrecords.com/world-records/most-broken-bones-in-a-lifetime.

4. "Legendary Evel," Evel Knievel, Accessed November 18, 2018. http://evelknievel.com/the-man/.

Chapter 12: Sold Out

1. J. Wesler, "Federal Policies Affecting Airport Noise Compatibility Programs," International Air Transportation Conference, 1981. doi:10.2514/6.1981-829.

2. Kyle Idleman, *Not a Fan: What Does It Mean to Really Follow Jesus?* (Grand Rapids: Zondervan, 2013), 32.

CPSIA information can be obtained
at www.ICGtesting.com
Printed in the USA
JSHW031107120720
6612JS00001BA/13